"Probably one of the top ten books ever written. I can't wait to read it."

—JEFF FOXWORTHY

"These guys are better than Steinbeck. This book should be canonized. It's better than most of the New Testament."

—DON MILLER, *NEW YORK TIMES* BESTSELLING AUTHOR OF *BLUE LIKE JAZZ*

"Tripp and Tyler are two of the funniest people I've ever met in my life. (I haven't met Jim Gaffigan yet, but if I do, they told me I can change this endorsement.) This book is hilarious and will have you looking at situations in life completely differently. Most notably, why the people enhancing their already complicated coffee at Starbucks insist on blocking the only trash can in the entire establishment."

—JON ACUFF, *NEW YORK TIMES* BESTSELLING AUTHOR OF *START*

Stuff
You Should
Know About
Stuff

Stuff
You Should
Know About
Stuff

How to Properly Behave in Certain Situations

Tripp & Tyler

BenBella Books, Inc. • Dallas, TX

BenBella Books, Inc.
10300 N. Central Expressway
Suite #530
Dallas, TX 75231
www.benbellabooks.com
Send feedback to feedback@benbellabooks.com

Printed in the United States of America
10 9 8 7 6 5 4 3 2

Library of Congress Cataloging-in-Publication Data is available for this title.
ISBN 978-1-939529-68-8

Editing by Glenn Yeffeth and Katie Kennedy
Copyediting by Eric Wechter
Proofreading by Michael Fedison and Cape Cod Compositors, Inc.
Illustrations by Kevin J. Keigley
Cover art and design by Josh LaFayette
Text design and composition by Ralph Fowler
Printed by Lake Book Manufacturing

Distributed by Perseus Distribution
www.perseusdistribution.com

To place orders through Perseus Distribution:
Tel: (800) 343-4499
Fax: (800) 351-5073
E-mail: orderentry@perseusbooks.com

Significant discounts for bulk sales are available. Please contact Glenn Yeffeth at glenn@benbellabooks.com or (214) 750-3628.

There are a lot of unwritten rules in the world today. This is our attempt to write them down, and in doing so, make the world a more tolerable place.

Contents

Preface

In the event that you hate this book, here are a few tips to help you feel better about the purchase that you now regret:

○ Did you know that shaving razors will last for months if you just dry them off after using them? Seriously, they're not getting dull—they're just rusting.

○ To quickly convert Celsius to Fahrenheit, just multiply by two and add thirty.

○ If you've accidentally written on a dry-erase board with permanent marker, just take a dry-erase marker and draw over the permanent markings. Then take a dry cloth and wipe away. Good as new.

○ To make a room-temperature can of soda—or adult beverage—ice-cold in minutes, just put it in a pot and cover with ice. Then add two cups of salt and fill pot with water. Wait three minutes and your beverage will be ice cold.

○ Get rid of a brain freeze by pressing your tongue against the roof of your mouth. Same goes for preventing a sneeze. And I bet the same goes for another thing.

Public
Situations

Rules for My Waiter

We don't need a buddy

No offense, but I need you to be my waiter, not my pal. I don't need you to squat down to get on my level. My neck can handle looking up for a half-minute. And don't you dare slide in the booth with me.

"Hungry? There's an app for that. I kid!"

You're not better than me

Hey, Xander (that's always his name), don't scoff at me for not knowing what vegetable escabeche is. It's your job to know, not mine. Oh, and you should know that I'm basing your tip on a complex algorithm I designed that factors in how quickly you can explain it to me, whether or not a seven-year-old can understand it, your height, and your facial expression when I ask for the silverware you didn't give me. It usually comes out to be around 20 percent.

Sing

When it's my birthday, sing the song like you mean it or don't sing it at all. It's hard enough to follow along with your restaurant's custom rendition, but your apathy is making me depressed.[1]

You're not being timed

Spouting off today's specials like the Micro Machine guy[2] isn't helping anyone.

The Early Bus

I've never been a waiter, so there's a good chance I'll get reamed for this. But I'd like to propose a cute little rhyme that every waiter everywhere must learn. It goes like this:

> *If they've already paid,*
> *bus away.*

---

1. And I'm already plenty depressed from celebrating my birthday at a restaurant that sings to you.

2. Mr. Testaverde from *Saved by the Bell*.

But if they're still sitting down,
don't you dare start bussing the freaking table as
    though they're an inconvenience to you,
you selfish bastard.

I'm still tinkering with the rhyme scheme but I think the point remains.

Wring out your washcloth

As much as I typically love resting my elbows on a damp table, I think I'll pass tonight.

Two-second rule

When you bring me my check, wait at least two seconds to see if I'm pulling out a card. I shouldn't have to wait for you to come back.

Go ahead and fill my water

No need to ask. There's never a situation where I'd prefer a half-full glass over a full one.

Open Letter to Starbucks Patrons

Dear Starbucks patrons,

Please have a game plan before you even enter the store. Your time at the counter should closely resemble Seinfeld's encounter with the Soup Nazi. This is not the time to ask how fresh the bagels are or whether or not their beans are of the shade-grown, fair-trade variety. Simply state your order, hand them your money, and shimmy to the left without making eye contact.

No one is impressed with your complicated drink order. People with complicated drink orders always do two things: 1) They say their order really fast in order to mystify the barista with its one-of-a-kindness, and 2) They give a little half-smile/side-glance at the other people in line to make sure they know who the boss is around here. I got news for you, guy—the rest of us caffeine-deprived people in line are hoping you accidentally spill your venti triple-shot no-foam skinny mocha chip latte with peppermint drizzle on the inseam of your pleated khakis.

Please be reasonable with the volume of your voice. Here's a hint: It shouldn't resemble your "at a football game voice" or your "reuniting with a childhood friend voice." If you're unsure of what this sounds like, just look around. The rest of us seem to have it down pat.

Please share the plug love. Hey, guy who always monopolizes the only outlet in the entire store—the other seven of us working on nearly dead laptops are conspiring to stuff your charging smartphone into the burr grinder.

Please don't make me have to do a Kareem Abdul-Jabbar[3] sky-hook to throw away my trash. I understand that you need to dress your coffee up a little bit, but you don't have to box me out like you're Walter White dropping chemicals into a beaker. There's only one trash can in the entire place, and it's underneath that six-inch hole you've been guarding for the past five minutes.

Please don't pull two tables together so you'll have room for your computer and multiple stacks of papers while other people, hypothetically, have to try to work while kneeling against a wall, which caused them to tweak something in their lower back . . . which caused it to now hurt when they bend down and tie their kids' shoes this morning.

---

3. I tried to think of a more up-to-date sports reference here, but I think the hook shot went away in the NBA around the same time as thigh visibility.

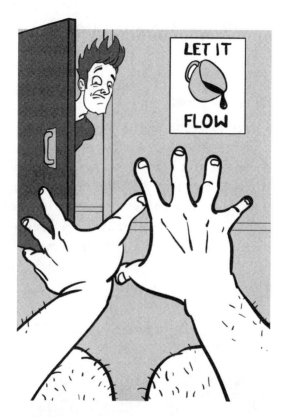

Lastly, please lock the onesy. You know, the onesy—it's the public restroom made for only one person at a time. There's a lock for a reason. This is the single worst situation to make eye contact with another person.

Sincerely,
Tripp and Tyler

Movie Commandments

Thou shalt leave a seat buffer

When guys go to the movies together, the seating dilemma always arises. Do I choose the seat right next to him? I don't want him to get the wrong idea. Should I leave a seat in between? Will that appear homophobic? Let me clear this issue up once and for all. Leave a buffer. No one has ever gotten mad about extra elbow room. If it's crowded, act like you're saving it for someone else. Or, like me, you can obsess over sitting down first so your friend has to make the decision.

Thou shalt be reasonable with what you're sneaking in

We're all doing it. But some of us are getting a little too cocky with our contraband. A twenty-ounce Coke, Sour Patch Kids, gin and tonic . . . all perfectly reasonable. A salad, breadsticks, and Never-Ending Pasta Bowl from Olive Garden, though, is going to ruin it for all of us.

Thou shalt never miss previews

The previews are just as important as the movie itself (if not more). I've broken a number of traffic laws and ruined several friendships just to make sure I get there to see them. If I happen to miss them, I sink into a mild depression that lasts at least a third of the movie.

Thou shalt not look at me during the movie

I like to grab a handful of popcorn, start at the heel of my hand (with the majority of the handful resting on my nose), and funnel the popcorn into my chomping mouth.[4] No one dared me to do it like that. I just like it that way. So please, eyes forward. That's why it's dark in here. What happens in a movie theater stays in a movie theater.

---

4. The post-movie walk into the lobby is always a little embarrassing as the light finally reveals the collection of kernels all over my torso.

Thou shalt shut your freaking mouth

Under no circumstances is it okay to tap me on the shoulder and ask me where you've seen that actor before. That's what IMDb is for. I specifically invited you in hopes that there would be no social interaction whatsoever. How rude.[5]

"OH! That's that guy from that one episode of that one show! I love him!"

Thou shalt never get up

I would rather get a bladder infection or even soil my pants a little than go to the bathroom during the middle of a movie. Not only do you miss out on some key plot development, but with how much you paid for your ticket, those precious three minutes come out to be worth around $7.

---

5. Made you think of Stephanie Tanner, didn't we?

Concert Etiquette

• •

Ah, concerts. The cultural enigma of paying exorbitant amounts of money to stand next to complete strangers and listen to less-polished versions of your favorite illegally downloaded MP3s.

Here are a few crucial do's and don'ts when attending one of these music shows.

○ First of all, no matter what show you're at, big or small, one thing's for sure—you're going to be tempted to sing along. And, that's okay. Just remember no one is as impressed as you are with how well you've memorized the lyrics.

○ If the song being performed isn't one that involves dancing, please—please—don't be the reason we are all standing. We didn't buy tickets so we could burn calories. There are plenty of other ways to express how big of a fan you are, like . . . being in attendance.

○ Yelling out a song title you want to hear has a .019 percent chance of working,[6] which is roughly the

---

6. From the Oxford Dictionary:

> **set list** Syllabification: (set list) *Noun* a list of the songs that a band or singer intends to perform at a particular concert.

same odds as the person next to you congratulating you for knowing such an obscure song.

○ If you yell out "Freebird," everyone around you wants to punch you in the neck. Seriously. They literally want to paralyze your vocal chords so they won't have to hear you say it thirty-eight more times throughout the night.[7]

○ Remember back in 1996 when that clever guy brought a laser pointer and shined it on the Gin Blossoms? That was hilarious. That one time.

○ If you're tempted to call a friend and hold up your phone and make them jealous for not being there, just know that what they're hearing sounds more like a pterodactyl impersonating a modem than their favorite song.

○ Oh, and a quick word to the band: Easy on the new songs. They're not why we came.

○ One hundred dollars says you're going to regret buying that thirty-dollar tour schedule T-shirt on the way out.

---

7. If there's one thing we know about Freebird Guy, it's that he never requests it just once.

◯ And another hundred says that you'll never even once go back and watch that shaky footage you insisted on shooting on your iPhone.

Reasons a Japanese Steakhouse Isn't Worth the Hassle[8]

....

The Shrimp Toss

Having a Japanese chef toss a shrimp in your mouth is incredible when you're twelve. It's less incredible when you're on a date with your wife. And to all the chefs out there—once it's bounced off my top lip and onto the floor, there's no need to keep trying. I've already lost my dignity. Please stop kicking me while I'm down by adding more sauce marks to my face.

Seating

A Japanese steakhouse is arguably the worst place to go for a group outing. If you don't race ahead, you'll end up getting stuck at the right-angle corner next to the random guy who tries all night to get you to join his pyramid scheme. Look, Guy, I know it makes sense—everyone uses natural gas. What doesn't make sense is how you're not picking up on my signals. I've been reading this menu for the past half hour . . . and I already ordered.

---

8. NOTE: Tripp wanted to make sure you knew that he did not contribute to this section. He is steadfast in his love and devotion of the hibachi grill and is currently mad at Tyler for speaking negatively about the onion volcano.

Language Mix-ups

There needs to be some kind of rule about restaurant workers in America knowing at least a basic level of English. Last time I went I asked for an extra napkin and I was treated to a double shot of rice wine and a lower back massage,[9] How are we getting these things confused? To be clear, I'm not mad about it;[10] I'm just a little afraid of what asking for a refill might get me.

Acting Surprised at the Volcano

I don't have the heart to tell the chef that no one has been impressed with the onion volcano since 1993. He's still so proud of it. He's like the uncle that still pulls quarters out of your ear. Look, Uncle Danny, I'm twenty-eight. I know about the inner workings of an ear, okay? I would have felt metal grazing my cochlea.

Extra Portion

I can't even enjoy the first half of my meal because I'm so worried about who's getting the extra portion of fried rice. As soon as the chef begins to scoop up that last helping, I'm trying to discreetly box out my neighbors and solidify

---

9. FYI: Next time you're at Yakiniku, order "another napkin." It will revolutionize your dining experience.

10. Is this the correct use of a semicolon?

intense eye contact, even though I know deep down he's going to give it to the cute blonde who won't eat it.

Cultural Offenses

Never again will I make the mistake of asking for a fortune cookie. You would have thought I'd punched a child in the face. No, hibachi grills do orange sherbet, thank you very much—perfect for those of us who want to polish off our four-course meal with a Push Pop.

Recommendations for the Next Hotel I Stay In

○ **Please start washing the comforters.** We all know that earlier in the day, a naked, sweaty, fat man rested his taint on the comforter while he blow-dried his hair. I know you can neither confirm nor deny this, but the least you could do is have the housekeeper bring a new comforter to my door, shrink-wrapped[11] like an airline blanket.

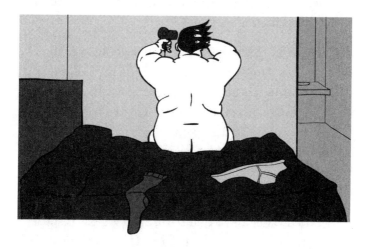

---

11. If you shrink-wrapped a turd, I'd at least consider handling it.

○ **Please choose an appropriate height for your shower head.** If a 5'11" man wants to rinse the shampoo out of his hair, under no circumstance should he have to do a naked wall sit in order for that to happen. Naked wall sits should be reserved for the privacy of one's own home.

○ **Please choose a shampoo that doesn't smell like a condiment.** I have a feeling that the selection of the shampoo/conditioner/body wash combo is a pretty big decision. Just make sure the person with the final say isn't suffering from a cold or a recurring olfactory injury. I can't afford to go into that two o'clock meeting with my skin smelling like I just bathed in Hollandaise sauce.

○ **Please have a variety of pillows.** If you're going to spend the money to have twelve pillows on my bed, at least throw a little variety in there. For those of us who like our pillows to feel like two pieces of cardboard stacked atop one another, sleeping on a pillow that resembles a rolled-up sleeping bag is an impossible task.

○ **Please be reasonable with the price of mini-fridge items.** Your $7 bottled water and $4 Fun Size Snickers Bar is starting to make the movie theater feel like a thrift store.

○ **Please don't give me a guilt trip about not wanting to reuse my towel.** If you're really trying to save money,[12] just add that eleven cents worth of water you had to use to my bill.

○ **Please destroy all mini-coffee makers.** Chances are, the only people who are desperate enough to get up and make coffee in their hotel room are also raging (and sometimes belligerent) caffeine addicts. Speaking on behalf of those addicts, a pot the size of a shot glass isn't going to cut it.

○ **Please get rid of the pamphlet tower.**[13] No, it's not bothering me. I just feel sorry for it. It just sits there alone underneath the pay phones, desperate for someone to come make a collect call.

○ **Please trust me with your hangers.** I promise I won't steal your clothes hangers. Seriously. All you're doing by permanently attaching them to the closet rod is causing people to want them more. Oh, and while we're at it, now you're sewing pillows onto your chairs? Is throw pillow theft a bigger deal than I'm aware of?

---

12. This is about saving money, isn't it? You can't expect me to believe this is about the environment.

13. Are all hotel pamphlets required to advertise either gemstone quarries, local waterfalls, or tubing?

○ **Please stop insisting that your $12.95 breakfast buffet is a great deal.** I don't know what you think the going rate is for limp bacon and bouncy eggs, but you're shooting a tad high. I know, I know—you think it's worth it because you have that cool conveyer belt toaster and endless supply of batter cups for the waffle maker, but you're wrong. At least trick me into thinking it's free and sneak that $12.95 into the price of my bottled water.

○ **Please choose a shower faucet that idiots can figure out.** If I have to spend more than 1.5 seconds figuring out A) how to turn the water on, or B) how to make it hot, you've chosen the wrong one. It is never acceptable for me to have to use two hands at this point in my showering process.

○ **Please chill out with the shower caps.** I'd be willing to bet my life savings that the only people in the world who still use shower caps have packed their own. There is no need for them to be standard issue right next to my mini-bottles of shampoo, body lotion, and mouthwash. Put all that money you'll save toward giving that comforter an extra wash or two.

The Inadvertent Doorman

••

Question: When entering a restaurant, how close should a person be for you to hold the door open for him? You know what I'm talking about:

> MY THOUGHTS
> (having just walked through
> a door)
> Oh look—someone's coming. I think
> I'll hold the door open for him.
> After all, that's the kind of guy
> I am.

> GUY'S THOUGHTS
> That guy couldn't be holding the
> door open for me, could he? I'm
> like sixty yards away.

> MY THOUGHTS
> Hmm. That guy's a lot farther
> away than I thought. This was a
> mistake. Is it okay to unhold the
> door?

> GUY'S THOUGHTS
> Do I need to walk faster? What's
> the proper etiquette here? Does
> he expect me to jog?

MY THOUGHTS

I don't think he sees me. I think
it's okay to unhold as long as we
don't make eye con— Damn. We just
made eye contact. I think I'm
stuck here for the long haul.

GUY'S THOUGHTS

Wait, is this guy mad at me? He
seems mad. How do I feel guilty
right now?

MY THOUGHTS

Would looking at my watch be too
obvious? There has got to be a
way to speed this up.

GUY'S THOUGHTS

Is he actually pulling the watch-
look? People do that? There's no
way he cares about what time it
is. He's just messing with me.
I'll show him. Whoops—looks like
I need to tie my shoe . . . right
now.

MY THOUGHTS

No! What the . . . okay, is
he? . . . I've never hated
anyone as much as this guy.

GUY'S THOUGHTS

Let's see, I think I'll just twirl
the ol' keys a little, just to
make sure he understands how
little of a hurry I'm in.

                    MY THOUGHTS
Are you kidding me!? You bastard!
Release me from this bondage!

                    GUY'S THOUGHTS
Okay, here we go. It's time to
enter.

                    MY THOUGHTS
Almost done here. You've done
well. Just exchange pleasantries
and be on your way.

                      GUY
Hi. How's it going?

                      ME
Nothing much.

Public Restroom Etiquette

have friends who flat-out refuse to use public restrooms. Don't get me wrong—I understand their hesitation. But the experience doesn't have to be that bad. There are just a few things you have to keep in mind:

1. **Know when reading is acceptable.** I have learned the hard way that it is not acceptable at Barnes & Noble to take a book off the shelf and into the bathroom with you. Apparently, a book that has been taken into a bathroom by a previous reader is spoken for in the same way that a home that has been the site of a gruesome basement murder is. Starbucks, however, is fair game.[14]

2. **Leave a generous cushion while waiting.** There isn't a man on the planet who appreciates another male lurking a foot behind him at the urinal. You want to leave the maximum amount of space behind the urinal-user while still making it clear to the person who's just entered that you're next in line. It's one of life's most difficult balances.

---

14. At the very least, you should tuck the book/newspaper into the back of your waistband before entering. Have some self-respect.

3 **Check the toilet paper first.** Guess what's worse than being out of toilet paper at home?

4 **Kick Flush.** I would rather touch the rotting carcass of a duck than the silver flush handle on a public toilet. If I'm not able to karate kick high enough to get the job done, the next patron is walking into a surprise. I know I'm not the only one. We're the reason automatic sensor flushers were invented.

5 **Wash hands if someone is looking.** This is the one time in life where I succumb to peer pressure from people I don't even know. If I don't wash my hands,[15] I feel like they're going to follow me to my table and tell everyone who I'm sharing chips with what just happened. If I'm ever in there with a friend, I stand back a little and let him take the lead. If he washes, I step up and pretend that's what I had planned all along.

6 **Know when to hold it.** In the event that you enter a onesy and get bear-hugged by a palpable, eye-watering stench, there's only one option: Hold it and develop a minor intestinal problem rather than risk having the stench embed itself in your clothes.[16]

---

15. No need, remember? I kick-flushed.

16. It will.

Urinal Etiquette

••

Urinal: a wall-mounted toilet for men to pee in or little boys to do whatever they want in. Home to pink disks that no one has ever touched.

Ladies, did you know men have another toilet option for going number one? It's true, but I'm not sure why. We all know that 99 percent of the time a person (man or woman) is either going number one or going both. And, I don't know any men who halfway through a number two get up, walk to the urinal, use it, and then return to a sitting position on the regular toilet. Just proving that doing a number one doesn't require a urinal. Not to mention, most homes don't have them.

And men, can we please get on the same page with how we act at said urinal? It's embarrassing.[17] Here are some much-needed tips to guide you in your next experience.

❶ Under no circumstance is it okay to make eye contact with another urinal user. Conversation is okay, but only while looking straight ahead.

---

17. More embarrassing than that pee spot you get when under-shaking (see #5 on next page).

❷ Please pee at an angle to avoid splashing. If you're not aware that you're splashing, wearing flip flops next time may convince you otherwise.

❸ Under no circumstance should you rest your forearm on the wall above the urinal. Are you this tired?

❹ No high-fives or handshakes.

❺ It's important to find a good shaking balance— too few, pee spot. Too many, you'll start to arouse suspicion.

❻ Pants down past the knees without realizing the absurdity? Not okay. Pants down past the knees in an attempt to be hilarious? Celebrated.

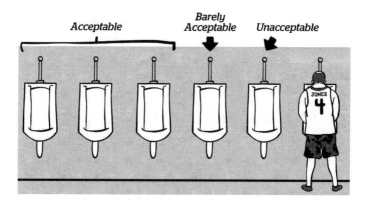

Public Pool Disclaimers

....

After spending the afternoon at a neighborhood pool the other day, I've decided I'm going to write a letter to the American Public Pool Administration. In it, I'm going to propose that the following list of disclaimers be hung on the entrance gate of every public pool in America.

Before entering this aquatic area, you must accept the following:

1. Our Kiddie Pool consists of 25 percent water, 70 percent chlorinated urine, and 5 percent disseminated fecal matter. Chances are, earlier this afternoon someone dropped their kids off at the pool and those kids did the same. But don't worry, we got most of it out with that leaf scraper thing.

2. There is no set Adult Swim schedule. We go by the teenage lifeguard's Arbitrary Whim System (AWS), which seems to be working well thus far (for him).

3. There is a direct correlation between the size of a person and how much skin they will expose. The greater the surface area, the greater the chance that you'll throw up in your mouth before the day is over.[18]

---

18. It's okay. Remember the leaf scraper thing?

We don't swim in your toilet, so don't pee in our pool.
Or do.
Either way.
Everyone does it though, so you'd actually be in the **minority** if you didn't.

Just saying...

❹ There is an above-average chance your kid's toy will be stolen—not permanently, but at least for the duration of your stay. If the redhead with freckles takes it, we suggest just sucking it up and diving for coins instead. He's here unsupervised . . . again.

❺ If you're thirsty, we have rusted Coke machines located near the restrooms. We hope you're in the mood for Diet Sprite, because everything else is sold out. Either that, or it's short-circuiting from all the wet dollar bills.

❻ Don't mind the teenage couple making out. This is the only place they could get some privacy. That innocent game of Spider will turn into something scandalous, so be prepared to go ahead and have "the talk" with your four-year-old.

7 Walking into our restrooms with bare feet is one of the biggest mistakes you can make during your time here, unless you appreciate the feel of warm, damp, hairy tiles beneath your feet.

8 Don't mind the older kids who will be playing a game that will inevitably hurt a bystander. This is just what they do. We, along with their parents, are intimidated by them.

9 Rest assured, there will be a kid you want to punch. These feelings are natural. But because of the guaranteed lawsuit that would follow your acting on this impulse, we recommend finding his dad and punching him instead—right in the part of his body responsible for creating such a monster.

Beach Etiquette

Hey, **Boom Box Guy,** please don't assume we all want to hear the same music as you. Or that we want to hear you sing along with it.

Let me yawn in peace

Yawning at the beach is now unsafe. If your mouth is open for more than a second, the dude next to you will have managed to coat your tonsils with the spray sunscreen that he's unsuccessfully applying to his back. (Just point it behind my head and spray, he thinks.) I recommend sporting a doctor's mask. Sure, the doctor's mask tan is a little more embarrassing than the sunglasses tan, but at least you'll be able to taste your shrimp scampi that night.

Learn to skim board in the privacy of . . . somewhere else

Hey, guy, guess who I don't want blocking my view? You. I didn't drive six hours with three screaming children to sit here and watch you unsuccessfully skim board for three hours. I would move my chairs, my umbrella, the 47 toys, the cooler, my four books, my three sons, and the baby pool, but it just seems more practical for you to relocate. Oh, and from the looks of things, you should consider sticking with bodysurfing.

Sunscreen will always be an issue

See illustration on page 142.

Reapplying sunscreen will always be an issue

We all have the same internal struggle after we go in for lunch. Do I really need to reapply my sunscreen? I just put it on two hours ago. I didn't get in the water, but I did sweat a little. What's the half-life of Banana Boat? We end up sucking it up and going through the application process all over again.

Learn how to throw

Hey, QB1, if your football lands near my son again, I'm going to get out of the pool (yes, actually get out) and stab it several times with that bottle opener that inexplicably came with my board shorts.

When leaving the beach, always rinse off with the hose

That, or just go get in the pool.

Burdens of Shopping

Putting Clothes Back on Hangers

I just found out that it's not acceptable, when you've decided you don't like an item, to just drape it over the rack or place it on the ground next to where it went. Who knew? I'll tell you who. My wife.

>   MY WIFE
> Where did that go?
>
>   ME
> Where did what go?
>
>   MY WIFE
> That shirt you just threw on the
> ground.
>
>   ME
> Um, placed on the ground.
>
>   MY WIFE
> You're supposed to put it back on
> the hanger.
>
>   ME
> Good one. Don't you know they
> have people for that?

```
                MY WIFE
        (walks away embarrassed)


                ME
What? Are you going to get the
people?
```

Getting Out of a Department Store

Before I can get to my car, I have to navigate through the human maze known as Macy's. I feel like I'm on *The Truman Show* and the store owners are just watching me try to make sense of it all. I think there were purses when I came in. How can the parking lot be on this level? I thought it was downstairs. These doors look right. No, it wasn't purses . . . it was scarves. I remember smelling perfume. Wait, I think we parked at Dillard's.

Accidentally making eye contact with someone who works at a mall kiosk

Showing the Receipt

This is the most unnecessary hoop that you have to jump through . . . in life. Before you can leave Walmart, you must first hand an elderly man a four-foot-long receipt with no less than seventy-five items. After looking at it for 0.25 seconds, he'll give your cart a passing glance, and notarize the encounter with a pink highlighter. Is this the best they could come up with as a last line of defense?

Speaking of Walmart . . .

Customer Service

I've only seen one Walmart employee smile. Come to find out it was because her shift was almost over. For some odd reason, these people have grown to hate life more than toll booth workers. How did this happen?[19]

---

19. Wait. I just remembered. It's because they work at Walmart. Sorry. I blanked there for a second. You know how they call Mesopotamia the Cradle of Civilization? Well, Walmart is the anti-Mesopotamia. It's the Cradle of Hell and Unhappiness.

Acceptable Places to Litter

In addition to the airplane seatback pouch,[20] here are a few other places where it's still okay to discard your trash.

○ **Movie Theaters.** There's something so freeing about finishing a movie in a theater . . . and just walking away. You enter the room heavy-laden, a tub of popcorn in one arm and a tub of Dr Pepper in the other, and leave burden-free. If you think about it, you're actually helping out the employees by giving them something to do in addition to interrupting the movie with the red light saber to count the number of people in the theater.

○ **Friend's Truck Bed.** If anyone deserves this, it's your truck-friend. He always gets out of driving.[21]

○ **Recycling Bin.** And then there are those times where you just can't muster up enough energy to walk all the way to the trash can, so you just toss it in the recycling bin instead, hoping to pull a fast one on the guys down at Waste Industries.

---

20. See page 117.

21. Except that one time a year when he helps you transport a giant file cabinet to your storage unit.

○ **Under Sand at the Beach.** This is essentially a DIY landfill, right? You're just skipping the middleman.

○ **From Any Bridge That Is So High That the Joy You Get from Watching the Item[22] Fall and Shatter Outweighs Any Potential Damage It Will Have on the Environment.**

---

22. Item should at least be the size of a desktop computer.

Surviving the Doctor's Office Waiting Room

....

The doctor's office waiting room is arguably the most miserable room on the planet. More miserable than a room that plays Nickelback's "Photograph" on an endless loop. More miserable than a room where you have to listen to two people argue politics or theology. Even more miserable than a room where you are forced to converse with Bill Belichick for fifteen minutes while he cuts the sleeves off of his sweatshirts.

I think the experience could be enhanced, though, if we went about things a little differently. Which is why we've come up with this list of ways to make this inevitable experience a notch more tolerable.

1 Thou shalt record your time of arrival as one minute earlier than the person who got there before you.

2 Thou shalt not offend the receptionist by actually speaking to her. She has way more important things to do . . . like make yet another photocopy of my insurance card.

③ Thou shalt not make eye contact with other patients, especially if you're at the OB-GYN with your wife and you see the high school girl that babysits your kids.

④ Thou shalt choose your chair wisely. Arbitrarily switching seats for no apparent reason is more awkward than the face nipple on that guy sitting across from you.

⑤ Thou shalt suck it up and read WebMD and Type II Diabetes pamphlets until that bastard surrenders the room's only *US Weekly*. Oh, and if he tries to take it back into the room, thou shalt take any measure to prevent that from happening.

⑥ Thou shalt not talk[23] to anyone. 'Tis better to appear rude than get in a discussion about the reason you're there.

⑦ Thou shalt pay your co-pay with confidence, even though you're not entirely sure what a co-pay is.

---

23. If the silent treatment fails, detailing any problem between your waist and mid-thigh is the quickest way to terminate any conversation.

Observations from My Recent Trip to the Gym

○ The sauna is not the place to do some extra crunches. I came in here to relax and not administer CPR to your soon-to-be lifeless body.

○ Why is everyone walking around with gallon milk jugs of water? Are you worried about getting stranded?

○ If you're naked in the locker room, at least pretend that you're in a hurry to get dressed. Note: This is not the time to prop your foot up on the counter and clip your toenails.

○ When you don't know what to do, head over to the water fountain.[24]

○ Keep telling yourself you're going to use those racquetball courts one day.[25]

---

24. Also works if you're thirsty and didn't bring your own gallon jug.

25. You won't. You're not going to go buy a racquet, goggles, and a sleeve of balls just so you can play with a stranger you met in the steam room.

○ I can't imagine the wondergel[26] in the shower is performing any one of its intended functions well.

○ I know you love your new studio-quality Beats by Dre headphones. Is the treadmill the ideal place to wear them? I'm seriously asking.

○ If I'm being honest, my $30/month is essentially a hot tub membership. Kind of annoying, though, that I have to walk through a gym to get to it.

○ There seems to be an inverse correlation between the amount of time someone spends doing curls in front of the mirror and the amount of time I'd want to hang out with him.

---

26. You know, the shampoo/conditioner/soap/body gel/lotion/aloe vera/lip balm/sunscreen/fabric softener/condiment concoction in a single dispenser in every shower stall.

Situations
Involving
Communication

Phone Rules

Check it to my face

When we're sitting together at a table, what makes you think you're being discreet when you check your phone under the table? Sinking your chin into your neck, frowning, and glancing south can only mean one thing. Okay, two things, but in that case I'd rather you were checking your phone.

Keep away-message brief

Enough with the instructions for how to leave a voice-mail. I've yet to find myself in a panic, wondering what to do after you've apologized[1] for not answering your phone. Was it name, then number? Will they get back to me as soon as they can?

If possible, let's just text

The single best thing about smartphones is not having to talk on them. So, if what you need can be wrapped up in a couple sentences, just text it. You'll like the result much better.

Allow me to be away from my phone

"Where have you been? I've called like three times and left two messages! Are you okay?! Did I do something wrong? Are you avoiding me?" Hold on a minute, psychopath. I just went to the bathroom—number one, mind you—and was only away from my phone for forty-five seconds. From here on out, you should probably get used to me declining your calls.

---

1. Why the apology? Why all the "sorry I can't answer the phone right now"? The only thing you should be apologizing for is not putting a half-second worth of original thought into your away-message.

You're the only one who cares about your new ringtone

You know when your phone starts ringing, or should I say blaring that new Katy Perry track, and you wait an extra second or two to answer it so that everyone around you hears it? Yeah, you're the only one who likes that. The rest of us use the vibrate feature like adults.

Excuses When You See Someone You Haven't Called Back

••

One of the most awkward situations in life is running into a person who has left you a message that you haven't returned. Most of the time they will just pretend like the phone call never happened. Other times, though, they'll stare deep into your soul and broach the subject with vigor.

Have no fear though. Just choose one of these excuses:

❶ **"Did you get a new number?"** You must say this phrase while pulling out the phone to scroll through recent calls with a confused look on your face to ensure maximum believability. You're letting the person know that this was definitely a phone malfunction[2] ("Sometimes it does this," you insist) and was in no way intentional. Before this person can probe any deeper, you need to ask for the "new" number and start programming it in.

❷ **"I've been meaning to, but I've been so busy."** This is the lamest of excuses, but surprisingly acceptable. You

---

2. Even though he has the same phone as you and knows how preposterous it is for a single contact to disappear out of thin air, somehow he'll still believe it.

convey the notion that calling this person back has constantly been in the back of your mind, but you were physically incapable of making it happen. Giving this explanation requires the ability to do two things at once: While you say it, you must also be forming a list in your head of all the things that made you so busy.[3]

❸ **"I knew I'd be seeing you."** This is more of a panic reaction than a well-crafted excuse. Use this when you accidentally run into someone who is expecting a call back. Be careful of the context though. It can really backfire.

> NEIL
> Hey! Say, did you get that message I left you last month?
>
> ME
> Oh . . . yeah. I, uh, didn't call back 'cause I knew I'd be seeing you here. I was right!
>
> NEIL
> You knew you'd be seeing me at a grocery store . . . on a random Tuesday afternoon?

---

3. Anyone who is audacious enough to bring up the fact that you haven't called him back will ask you to list off what has been making you so busy. It might be a good idea not to have this kind of person in your life.

<pre>
          ME
Yes . . . I sure did. I know how
much you love groceries.

          NEIL
So when you heard my message,
you immediately thought, "Instead
of just calling Neil back, I'll
just drive up to Publix every now
and then and see if I don't run
into him."

          ME
Unconventional, huh?
</pre>

❹ **"I got a new phone."** Although you may not have gotten a new phone since the message was left, you have gotten a new phone at some point in the past. It's a stretch, but technically not a lie. You'd be surprised by its effectiveness.

Dropped-Call Etiquette

1 For the sake of those around you, keep the "Hello? Can you hear me? I can hear you . . . can you he— I can—You still there?" count to a maximum of four. And while we're at it, keep your voice's volume knob at "normal" instead of shouting to the other person as though she is Baby Jessica[4] trapped in the bottom of a well.

2 When you're in the middle of an extremely long rant about your last visit to the doctor and you don't hear any affirmation sounds coming from the other person, either your story is terrible and he's playing Candy Crush,[5] or the call was dropped twelve minutes ago when you were detailing your urinary tract infection.

3 When you do get reconnected, no need to spend the first two minutes of the resumed conversation justifying why it couldn't have been you who dropped

---

4. I made a promise to myself years ago that if I ever wrote a book, I'd have at least one Baby Jessica reference in it. Man of my word.

5. Or whatever app that adult iPhone owners are currently obsessed with. Point remains.

the call.[6] Arguing about who had more bars isn't moving this conversation along.

❹ One of the most difficult decisions to make is whether or not to call back if the call was dropped during the conversation wrap-up. You should come up with a special code phrase—ours is "Snowplow Huckabee"—that signifies "Our essential business is done, so if we get cut off after this, there's no need for a call back."

❺ If you are on the receiving end of the tedious story (mentioned above) and you get reconnected, he'll inevitably ask where he was in his story. You, of course, weren't listening, so the only safe response here is "toward the end." Letting him decide will only result in your having to listen to the story all over again.

❻ Let's limit the number of reconnecting attempts to three. If you still can't make it work after three, it's obvious that the conversation wasn't meant to happen. Send a quick text or email later if it was really important, but at this point, who cares?

---

6. Who had AT&T? That's all you need to know.

You're Doing Email Wrong

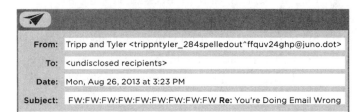

From:	Tripp and Tyler <trippntyler_284spelledout^ffquv24ghp@juno.dot>
To:	<undisclosed recipients>
Date:	Mon, Aug 26, 2013 at 3:23 PM
Subject:	FW:FW:FW:FW:FW:FW:FW:FW:FW **Re:** You're Doing Email Wrong

If your email contains "FW:" in the subject line, you're doing it wrong. There's nothing that makes me want to delete an email before it even has a chance to load more than seeing that in my inbox.

If I have to scroll through at least 17 previous senders' master lists of email addresses before getting to the actual content, you're doing it wrong.

If there is an animated American flag that symbolizes how patriotic you are and how patriotic I could be if I forward this email to my list, you're doing it wrong.

>>>>>>>If all of the content
>>>>>>>rests up against a bunch
>>>>>>>of these arrows, you're
>>>>>>>doing it wrong.

If you're still using an email address issued to you by your Internet service provider,[7] you're doing it wrong.

---

7. Nothing shows your age more than an "@bellsouth.net" email address.

If your reply all doesn't contain A) something pertinent to everyone on the list, or B) something universally hilarious,[8] you're doing it wrong.

And lastly, if you have more than two consecutive sentences containing an exclamation point or having chosen to increase the size of your multicolored, ALL CAPS Comic Sans, you're doing it wrong.

Tripp and Tyler

Made Up Business Title
Company Name
Mailing Address for some reason

(o) office landline
(m) cell number referred to as "mobile" number
(e) unnecessary redundant email address
(w) website that no one will visit
(t) twitter handle
(f) facebook page
(l) linked in profile

.,.:)•´¯`♥ Inspirational Quote about how life can be better if you do something other than what you're already doing ♥.,.:)•´¯`

More social media promotion
thishasnothingtodowiththecontentofthisemail.com

Something about a "Self-Published Book" I wrote

 companylogothatarrivedasanattachment.png

CIRCULAR 230 DISCLOSURE: If this email wasn't written to you, it's illegal for you to be reading it. But the thing is, if you are reading THIS, then you've already read the email. Which is why this entire paragraph is not only a giant digital eyesore, it's also pointless. Let's say you're a nosey jackass and you read this email on someone else's device while they weren't looking. What now? Are you going to report yourself to the authorities? Has a single court case ever even made mention of this particular paragraph? I guess we'll never know.[9]

---

8. There are four things that are always funny, no matter the circumstances:
   1) A kid swinging a bat into his dad's privates
   2) A person accidentally walking into a glass door
   3) A post-2008 Tripp & Tyler YouTube video
   4) An overweight person falling through a trampoline

9. Because we don't care enough to Google the answer.

Quit Using These Phrases

"World-Class"

As in, "Neil Calfman is a world-class chef." How is this being decided? This tells me nothing about Mr. Calfman, his cooking ability, or how he fares against chefs of other classifications. "World" isn't a class.

"5x Smoother Hair"

I found this on my Suave shampoo bottle this morning. Who is verifying this? Mine feels twice, maybe three times as smooth. But 5x?! Come on, Suave.

"30 days same as cash"

Mentioned at the end of every car commercial ever made, yet still commits the fallacy of equating periods of time with currency.

"No Trans Fat"

I know you think you understand this since Dr. Oz explained it on *Oprah* last year, but you don't. It means nothing.

What to Do When There's Awkward Silence

Look at phone

Before pulling it out of your pocket, give a mildly surprised look and quiet "hmm" at the fake phone vibration that has just occurred in your pocket. Pull it out, press a few buttons, and let out a brief chuckle at that funny "text" you just received.

Fake yawn

Nothing alleviates an awkward situation like a good old-fashioned fake yawn. The second that the silent tension begins to arise, let out a slow, exaggerated yawn (fist-to-mouth optional, though I've found it works well). This will cause the other person to forget all about the awkwardness and begin wondering what it is you're up to that makes you so tired. He'll most likely assume you've been out late the night before at some awesome party or concert. Double win.

Whistle

If you left your phone in the car and you're unable to muster up a fake yawn, just start whistling an old classic.[10] Important: Never make eye contact with the other person while you're whistling. This will ruin the moment entirely.

Study something

This one works anywhere. If you're sitting at Chili's, for example, and the awkward silence occurs, grab one of those cardboard coasters off the table and study its intricate design and composition. You must commit to this. Don't break away from your studies until the other person interrupts the silence.

Act interested in whatever is on the nearest TV

Unless the TV is more than twenty-five feet away. But honestly, why would you ever be more than twenty-five feet from a TV?

---

10. Otis Redding's "Sittin' on the Dock of the Bay," Don McLean's "American Pie," or Black Eyed Peas' "My Humps" have worked well for me.

Evite Tips

· ·

I f you've bought into "email" and you have more than three friends, then at one time or another you've received an Evite. But, do you know how to properly respond? Here are a few tips that may help:

❶ **Not leaving a response is the same as "maybe."** Nothing says "who gives a crap about this guy" like viewing an Evite without replying.

❷ **"Maybe" is the same as "no."** I'm willing to bet my wisdom teeth[11] that less than 1 percent of "maybes" ever show up.

❸ **Don't add guests if your reply is "no."** I shouldn't have to tell you this.

❹ **Adding more than two guests[12] is not acceptable.** There's probably a reason your other friends weren't invited.

❺ **Please use the carpool section so I can make fun of you later.**

---

11. I've put off having these removed for more than fifteen years anyway.

12. Unless you can add more than thirty without the party host noticing.

6 **Never be the first to reply.**   It's the same as publicly referring to someone as your "best friend."

7 **Your reply is not the time for movie quotes.**[13]   I don't know
how to explain this further.

---

13. See Beginner's Guide to Quoting Movies on page 83.

Rules Regarding Twitter

Here are a few tips to ensure your Twitter followers' experience is the best it can be.

○ **Retweeting a compliment about you is bragging.**[14] Adding a "Means a lot!" to the front end of it doesn't negate this fact. I promise that they'll feel just as thanked if you reply directly to them.

○ **Chill out on the hashtags.** Yes, I'm aware this is another way to make a witty joke, but the two minutes it takes to decipher where the spaces are supposed to go in your clever two-liner is time we simply don't have.

○ **Be conservative in your use of "my friend."** I've noticed a trend lately where people like to add "my friend"

---

14. The words "I'm excited" have become a means to talk about ourselves over Twitter in a way we wouldn't in a normal conversation.

Next time you're tempted to use these words try to rewrite the tweet without them, and then ask yourself:

- am I name dropping?
- am I bragging?
- does anyone care?

If the answer is yes, then consider writing a new tweet that has your reader more in mind. Or just brag, and don't pretend you're not.

Make sense?

Ok, I'm off to do something really important somewhere really exotic because my life is more exciting than yours, and I'm excited.

when referring to someone more popular or famous than them. I don't doubt the friendship, I just find it odd that you don't say the same about people on the popularity tier beneath you.

○ **Pimp your thing twice a day max.** This is completely arbitrary, I know, but I think we can all agree that once you've passed five, you're doing much more harm than good.

○ **Do tweet pictures.** It's a sneaky way to get 1,000 words out.[15]

○ **If you think you might be tweeting too much, you probably are.** You rarely hear anyone complaining that so-and-so doesn't tweet enough. PS: If they are saying that, it's a compliment.

○ **Tweet once about that awesome experience you're currently having.** The more times you tweet about it (i.e., type on your phone instead of experiencing said awesome thing), the less awesome it seems.

○ **Don't really tell us what you're doing.** An occasional status update is fine, but no one really cares that you're

---

15. Quit not using Instagram. There is no reasonable excuse for using another platform for your photos. (I'm looking at you, Lockerz with a "z.")

finally at work or that you are at lunch with really awesome people.[16]

○ **Do inspire us.** Say anything you want if it makes us laugh, think, cry, or rush to buy something. If you want to be a successful tweeter, then make the majority of your tweets about your followers— not you.

○ **Quit getting bent out of shape about changes to the privacy policy of this free service you voluntarily use.** Judging by the last few photos you posted from spring break, you're not too concerned with privacy anyway.

○ **Don't have two-way conversations with people on Twitter.** That is called "texting." You probably already pay a monthly subscription fee for that technology, and you should use it. Imagine if you were in a public place and two people were talking really really loud about where they were going to hang out later.

○ **Lastly, when jerks like us complain about how you're doing Twitter, just remind them about that fancy unfollow button and keep doing whatever you want.**

---

16. Nerve.com suggests that you should always ask yourself "Am I tweeting to love or be loved?"

Rules for the Facebook Profile Pic

○ If you're a guy, wear a shirt.

○ If you're a girl, be okay with the way you look from the front.

○ Under no circumstances should you pucker your lips (unless you're known for how well you can hold a pencil under your nose).

○ I know you think your head tilt looks sexy, but it actually just looks like you're standing at a window seat waiting to exit an airplane.

○ If you're someone I went to high school with, please don't use a picture of your kids as your profile pic. I'm sure your kids are great, but really I just want to know how much weight you've gained since graduation.

○ If you're going to take a selfie[17] in the mirror, you don't need a flash.

○ Don't hire a professional photographer unless your career requires a headshot.

○ Frequency—don't change it so often that I can tell when you get a haircut.

○ I shouldn't have to tell you this, but I should never get a notification that you've liked your own profile photo.

○ Don't feel the need to hold a small Haitian child in your arms to convince me you're a good person.

○ Don't use a microphone in your pic to subtly tell me you're important. I know you subbed as the keynote

---

17. Selfie 101: I shouldn't be able to see your extended arm in the foreground. Selfie 102: Quit taking selfies.

speaker at your son's middle school PTA assembly, but until you give a TED talk, leave the mic out of it.

○ There's a certain amount of time that it's okay to have your wedding photo as your avatar. Not exactly sure, just as long as it's changed by the end of your reception you should be fine.

○ The profile pic isn't the place to support a cause. You're only making me feel guilty. Also, the number

of causes that have been advanced by a banner on the lower third of a profile pic is equal to the amount of times I've arm-wrestled Vin Diesel and won. (Note: I've never defeated Vin Diesel in arm wrestling.)

○ Ask your friends first if the picture you're thinking of using is a good choice. Surely one of them will be honest with you. Better yet, give them some options—it could save the friendship.

PowerPoint Tips

f you're ready to present before people are ready to listen, just pretend to click something on the computer to cover up the fact that you don't know what to do with yourself.

○ Everything hinges on your first slide transition. If you've chosen something with an animation and/or a sound effect, it's over.

○ Unless your Google is broken, we should never see another piece of clip art.

○ There are better ways to hold someone's attention than reading a long paragraph exactly as it appears on the PowerPoint slide about a shocking statistic you just learned about, followed by all kinds of vague lingo that no one will remember two seconds from now, capped off by three bullet points.

○ Eighty-eight percent of all PowerPoint presentations will involve a technical difficulty[18] along the way. If you're unable to continue, maybe you shouldn't have been giving a presentation in the first place.

---

18. Add 12 percent if using Windows.

○ Desperately calling for an IT guy after banging a bunch of keys on your laptop is actually the most entertaining thing you've done so far.

○ Please.
Refrain.
From.
Going.
Through.
A.
Long.
List.
Of.
Facts.
One.
By.
One.
By.
One.
By.
One.

○ When you're finished presenting and you've asked if anyone has a question and no one says anything, you don't need to ask if they're sure. The dense silence is not them waiting to be convinced. It's time to dismiss.

Over/Under Guessing

Over/under guessers know just how to ruin your humble attempt at impressing them.

Normally you would never be willing to buy a pair of True Religion jeans. But, you just got a pair for $58 at a going-out-of-business sale. You can't wait to share with someone about this amazing deal.

                    YOUR FRIEND
          Hey there, Mr. Trendy Pants.

                    YOU
          Yeah, but YOU WON'T BELIEVE how
          much I got these for.

                    YOUR FRIEND
          Good deal?

                    YOU
          Guess how much I spent?

                    YOUR FRIEND
          I don't know . . . fifteen
          dollars?

You went bowling for the first time in two years, and as far as you can remember you've never had four strikes in one game before. You scored a 224.

> YOUR COMPETITIVE FRIEND
> How'd you bowl last night?

> YOU
>   (confident)
> Pretty good, I'd say.

> YOUR COMPETITIVE FRIEND
> Don't tell me you bowled over 250.

> YOU
> Um, okay I won't.

You are on a high, because at work today you made the sale of a lifetime.

> YOUR WIFE
> What's the big grin for?

> YOU
> Guess what happened at work today.

> YOUR WIFE
>   (excited)
> You finally got promoted to vice president of marketing!?

                    YOU
No . . . no I didn't get promoted.
In fact, I got fired. I have no
job and can no longer support our
family. And, I spent all of our
remaining money on a collectable—
it's the actual boat from the TV
series *Flipper.* Come look!
          (Wife starts to walk
          outside.)

                YOUR WIFE
          (crying)
Why would you—

                    YOU
Just kidding. I made a sale. Now
what have we just learned here?

Beginner's Guide to Quoting Movies

∙∙∙

1 **Watch your ratio.** At the very least, you should adhere to a 40-to-1 nonmovie-quote-to-movie-quote ratio. This is to prevent you from becoming the guy at a party who views every pause in a conversation as an opportunity to display his knowledge of the *Anchorman* script. As Mark Twain once said, "Movie quotes should pepper your conversation, not make your conversation taste like you've just sucked on a pepper tablet."[19]

2 **Keep it relatively mainstream.** There's nothing worse than being in a conversation with someone who starts quoting lines from deleted scenes of *Big Mama's House.*

3 **Use discretion with impersonations.** Unless you're impersonation is spot on, just go with your normal voice. Otherwise, your robotic "Smokin'!" will have the room wondering if you intended to show us what a British Arnold Schwarzenegger quoting *The Mask*[20] sounds like (in which case, you nailed it!).

---

19. Not that Mark Twain. The Mark Twain who used to live two doors down from me.

20. Hey, Chris. Remember how you bet me $200 that I couldn't work a *Mask* reference into the book? Pay up.

④ Variety is key. The last thing you want is to be labeled the "Napoleon Dynamite Guy." Don't get me wrong—it was a great movie. But you'd be surprised at how few social contexts call for a socially awkward "Tina, come get some ham!"

⑤ Get it right. Quoting movies can be risky. It takes a certain vulnerability to put oneself out there and quote a movie. Don't waste this moment by forgetting a word or trailing off at the end. Although it is amusing to the rest of us to hear you butcher the Baby Jesus prayer from *Talledega Nights,* you'll probably wish you'd avoided it altogether.

⑥ Christopher Walken is sacred ground. As a friend,[21] I would advise you to stay away from this one. It takes a skilled and masterful impersonator to pull off something that even resembles Walken. So if that's not you, show some respect and keep yours between you and your rearview mirror. If you can pull it off, however, you should seriously consider making that your normal, everyday voice.

---

21. If you bought this book, we consider you a friend.

Phone Books

∙∙∙

The other day someone suggested that I look something up in the phone book. Like, actually go get the phone book out of the cabinet and spend no less than seven minutes flipping through its reams of pages for a number that I'd then have to manually enter into my phone. Ugh.

I'm not sure what is being discussed behind closed doors at the Yellow Pages headquarters, but they've decided it's in everyone's best interest to keep pumping out phone books to every (Internet-friendly!) home in America. Though I don't understand their reasoning, I'm thankful that they're sticking with it. I've managed to find some other really great uses for phone books.

○ **Last-Minute Gift.** If you forget to get a gift for someone, all you have to do is follow these five simple steps. 1) Wrap up a phone book. 2) Give it to the person. 3) When he/she acts confused and disappointed, just say it's a joke. 4) Wait for the uproarious laughter to die down and tell him/her the real gift is on the way. 5) Forget to get that person a real gift.

○ **Free Booster Seat.** Who has $30 to spend on booster seats these days? For us, a Yellow Pages-and-a-half is the perfect height (the half,[22] obviously, serves as the backrest).

○ **Kindling.** Haven't enough trees been killed already? I say ditch the firewood and use wadded-up phone book pages instead. Sure, the fire will only last about thirteen seconds before you need to put on another page, but just think about how warm all of that ripping and wadding will make you.

○ **Display of Strength.** Now, I'm not suggesting you go around trying to prove how strong you are by attempting to rip phone books. No, I'm suggesting that you carry one around with you, and when you find someone with 60" biceps wearing a skintight Ed Hardy shirt, prove to him he's not as strong as he thinks he is. Sure, you got punched, but wasn't it worth it?

○ **Discipline.** You're sick. You thought I was going to suggest beating someone with a phone book, didn't you? Quite the contrary. I think a great punishment would be putting a tiny black dot next to one of the entries, closing the book, and making them listen to Beyonce's "Single Ladies" on repeat until they find it.

---

22. The White Pages.

Very Specific
Situations

Greeting Interception—What to Do?

Everyone has had this happen one time or another. Someone looks in your direction and offers up an enthusiastic greeting. You confidently fire back a pleasantry, only to hear the person behind you—the person who the initial greeting was intended for—hesitantly respond. What do you do now (after breaking into a full-body sweat, of course)? There really are only five options:

① **Turn Away.** Although this is our default reaction, use it in moderation. Turning away and pretending it never happened could potentially result in days (if not weeks) of self-loathing and regret. You're essentially admitting defeat. Like George Costanza and the "Jerk Store" debacle,[1] you'll be driving down the road a month-and-a-half later wishing you would have implemented one of the following four options . . .

❷ Continue the Conversation. This is a bit riskier, but following up the initial greeting with details about how your kids are and how busy your summer has been will undoubtedly result in the other person turning away and seeking out her original target in another aisle.

❸ Faux Bluetooth. The moment you realize you've intercepted the greeting, put your right hand to your right ear, look at whatever product is directly in front of you, and ask the phantom person on the phone if that was what they needed. Give the greeter a side-glance and a smile as you tell the person on the phone that you just wanted to double-check and you'll be home in a minute.

❹ Turn the Tables. This is advanced. It requires greater instincts and reflexes than hitting a Stephen

---

1. If you don't know about the "Jerk Store" debacle, please put this book down, Google it, watch it, and return to this book a better person.

Strasburg fastball.[2] Essentially, it's like pulling off the final act of *Inception* but without the help of Joseph Gordon-Levitt. The goal here is to talk past the greeter and make her think she is actually the one intercepting the greeting. There are so many factors involved here (volume, pitch, eye line, props, subject matter, facial expressions, etc.) that it is probably best to leave this to the seasoned veterans.

❺ **Shatter Something.**   If there is nowhere to turn, you're out of words, and both of your Bluetooth-less ears have been exposed, the only reasonable way out is to grab the nearest bottle and shatter it. Chances are, when the two or three shards of glass dig into her shin upon impact, she'll forget all about that embarrassing mistake you just made. Face. Saved.

---

2. His *2011* fastball (in case things don't work out like we thought).

Post Oil Change Conversation

••

                    LUBEMAN
            (approaches with a friendly
            smile)
        So, here's what we found.

                    ME
        Okay.

                    MY THOUGHTS
        But, really I just wanted to know
        where to sign. We already agreed
        on an $18.99 oil change.

                    LUBEMAN
        We changed your oil, and we
        noticed your air filter is
        preeeetty dirty, and you have a
        few hoses that could stand to be
        replaced.

                    MY THOUGHTS
        What step in changing my oil
        required you to open up my air
        filter?

                    ME
        Okay.

                    LUBEMAN
        And, see this (holds up another
        filter)—it's your blah blah blah

blah filter. It should only show
blah blah up to this blah blah,
and if you don't change it out,
blah blah blah could build up in
your blah blah blah and cause you
to have to replace your blah blah
and that gets really expensive.

MY THOUGHTS
There's no way in hell I'm falling
for this. It's a scam. My car
is fine. I just need an eighteen
dollar and ninety-nine cent oil
change.

ME
Okay.

LUBEMAN
Just sign here and we can get all
that taken care of for $96.89.
I didn't charge for your socket
connector valve. (Wink)

ME
Are you sure I need all this? I
mean . . .

LUBEMAN
You don't have to do it today, but
then you're at risk of paying a
lot more later. You could drive
out of here fine, but like I
said, you're blah blah could end
up clogging up your blah blah.

So . . . Want us to take care
of it?
    (Long pause)

        ME
    (defeated)
I do.

        LUBEMAN
I know.

Beginner's Guide to Tipping

Always double-fold

The quickest and most effective way to make your tip appear less meager than it really is (and to make yourself appear less stingy) is to fold it twice. This makes the tip feel more substantial, resulting in a much more pleasant three-second interaction with that person you'll never see again.

Go 20 percent or go home

Always, always, always tip a waiter 20 percent . . . unless he doesn't deserve it . . . or if you don't have it . . . or if the establishment he works for has predetermined his tip amount, which brings me to my next point . . .

No need to double-tip

If the restaurant where I'm dining is imposing the 18-percent-tip-included-for-parties-of-eight-or-more rule, who am I to argue? Look, guy. I'd go the extra 2 percent if I could, but The Man won't let me. And I have a pretty strict policy about obeying The Man when it works in my favor.

Online tips are legitimate tips

Domino's guy—the sole reason I tediously entered my debit card information online and tipped you there was so that we could avoid our weekly guilt-inducing stare down at my front door and, for once, engage in a clean pizza handoff. You know as well as I do that you were thanked in advance.

Share the love

There's an episode of *Curb Your Enthusiasm* where Larry David and Jason Alexander are eating lunch together. They split the bill down the middle, and then Larry asks Jason how much he's tipping (you know, to match him). Jason adamantly refuses to tell him. Don't be a Jason Alexander. Share the love.

Sorry, baristas

We don't tip the guy at Arby's for getting that roast beef sandwich just the way we want it, do we? No. We pay him the advertised price of a roast beef sandwich. Does a barista deserve more because he knows how to froth milk?[3]

Money is better than no money

This might be a direct contradiction to a number of things I've said above, but when in doubt (and there will always be times of doubt, no?), a little money is better than no money at all. I've yet to upset someone for handing him money. That dollar may not be a huge deal to me, but it could mean some sweet new ringtone to someone else.

A nonmonetary tip (i.e., advice) is only okay if it's really good[4]

---

3. Easy, baristas. I've heard your pro-tip arguments before. But no one is making you work there.

4. Feel free to use the tips in this book's Preface (page 11).

How to Know If You Should Throw Away a Shirt When Cleaning Out Your Drawers

••

Answering yes to any of the following questions means that you should immediately take the shirt out of your drawer and put it into a trash bag.[5]

O Have you worn it for 30 percent of the last year? If this is the case, you probably have a lot of people rooting for you to throw it away.

O Was it shot out of a gun?[6]

O Does it have a cartoonish V-neck? Look, V-necks are fine. But let's be honest—some of them look like you're wearing a short-sleeved cotton cardigan without an undershirt. It's offensive.

O Is it thicker than card stock? If it's providing your torso more insulation than a North Face parka, it

---

5. A trash bag that, once you get tired of stepping over it in the hallway, you'll place in the trunk of your car to take to Goodwill (but will put off until you have to transport a cooler).

6. Aka, is it an XXL?

ceases to be a T-shirt. I can't prove it, but I think these are somehow 200-percent cotton.

○ Does the thickness resemble one ply of toilet paper?

○ Does it have a witty or sarcastic phrase across the chest? A white-on-black "I'll procrastinate later" declaration isn't having the effect you intended, I promise you.

○ Is it embroidered?

○ Have you worn it less than three times in the last two years . . . and you don't have a gut feeling that you might wear it at some point in the future?

Appropriate Times to Cram

....

Before the Dentist

There's nothing quite like carving up your gums with dental floss the day before your dental appointment. No matter how delicate my approach, I end up with a mouthful of plaque-blood and gums so inflated that my son could use them as a pillow.

Then, to make matters worse, the dentist wants to talk about it:

>   DENTIST
> Have you been flossing?
>
>   ME
> I mean, I don't floss, like, every
> second of every day.
>
>   DENTIST
> Yeah, but on a regular basis?
>
>   ME
> Um, define "regular."
>
>   DENTIST
> Whoopsie—I think your top gum
> just popped. Never mind. I got my
> answer.

Before Shirtlessness

I'm going to a boat party this weekend and there's about a 100 percent chance that I'll do some push-ups in the bathroom before I take my shirt off. Some habits are just impossible to break. In high school I could pull off a thirty-minute workout routine in the bathroom, come out sweating, and convince everyone that something I ate just wasn't agreeing with me (and that I always remove my shirt when dropping a deuce).

Before Seeing Someone

If I'm going to meet up with someone that I haven't seen in a while, I'm going to spend about half an hour on his Facebook profile's About tab, relearning all the stuff he told me the last time we hung out and I immediately forgot.

Before a Test

Obviously.

Before We Have Guests Over

We have three kids, but my wife and I like to make our house appear as though we're childless whenever we have guests over. Every time it's the same—we pick up all the toys, hide the toys, buy some flowers, vacuum the carpet, mop the floor, steam clean the carpet, install new appliances, re-tile the bathroom, finish the basement, get our teeth whitened, and do a three-day juice cleanse. Then, when our guests arrive, we follow up our greetings with a casual apology that our house is such a wreck.

Checklist for Middle School Popularity in 1993

●●

Answering yes to any of the following criteria pretty much guaranteed top tier social status in middle school in 1993.

○ Is he rumored to not have a bedtime on school nights?

○ Did he fill in Mad Libs blanks with profanity or sexual references you'd never heard of?

○ Does he have a shaved-under bowl cut?

○ Is he currently in possession of a Ken Griffey Jr. Upper Deck rookie card?

○ Has he worn a Grandmama shirt this week?

○ Did he already know slang terms for that thing you just found out existed in Sex Ed?

○ Can he beat Mike Tyson's Punch Out without Game Genie?

○ Did he have a fitted baseball hat?

○ Did his parents let him watch *The Simpsons* and *In Living Color* on Sunday nights?

○ Does he at least seem like he knows the proper context of cuss words?

○ Did he covertly drink a tinfoil-wrapped Coke during lunch instead of a juice box?

○ Does he talk about having to shave?

○ Is he proud of never having read a single book?

○ Did he regularly quote[7] *Wayne's World*?

○ Had he haphazardly written all over the bottom leather portion of his JanSport book bag?[8]

○ Has he Frenched someone?

---

7. Quote frequency way more important than quote accuracy.

8. Note: Popularity contingent on using only one strap to carry book bag.

Inappropriate Times to Say "That's What She Said"

So You Decided to Become a Runner

ere are a few key pieces of advice you should keep in mind during your next jaunt.

○ **If you start with a long-sleeve shirt, end with a long-sleeve shirt.** Nothing is worse than taking off your long-sleeve shirt midrun, tying it around your waist, and continuing your run with a butt cape. Nothing. You'd look less foolish wearing a football helmet and an inner tube.

○ **Don't run in place while waiting to cross the road.** Besides looking ridiculous, you're wasting a precious gift. The stars have aligned to give you a couple of much-needed seconds to suck wind and talk yourself out of continuing. Take full advantage of this.

○ **Wait until the coast is clear.** Make sure there's no one around during your run-to-walk transition. If there's one thing in life that I don't want, it's for the people in that random '98 Acura Integra driving by to think I'm a quitter.

○ **Run with someone slower than you.** If you're anything like me, this might be a difficult task. You know when a fast walk turns into a quasi-jog? Yeah, that's my pace. But you're better off running alone than running with someone the slightest bit faster than you. Your entire run will be about trying to keep up with his pace, while he's six steps ahead of you, running backwards, telling you that you can do it in the most patronizing way possible.

○ **Beware of night walkers.** When running at night and you pass someone who is walking—not walking a dog, just . . . strolling—and he's not wearing athletic wear, there's a 100 percent chance he wants to murder you.

○ **Hide your keys in the safety zone.** In the history of running, there has only been one hiding place for a runner's keys—behind your car's front left tire. Even though every runner hides them here (and, surprisingly, thinks they're the only ones who thought of this location), thieves have collectively decided to give them a free pass.

Birthday Customs to Eliminate

s anyone willing to join forces with me in my quest to eliminate the following birthday customs?

○ **Cards.** There really are only two types of birthday cards out there—those that have money, and those that we wish had money. Think about how many hours of our lives we've wandered the card aisle looking for the perfect card, the one with words that

capture exactly what we want to communicate. Let me let you in on something—if I don't have to move a Hamilton or Jackson out of the way to read those words, the communication has already been done.

○ **"And Many More."** There are always a couple people at a party who have been enthusiastically waiting to cap off the group's performance of "Happy Birthday" with a performance of their own. It's only three words, and it's somehow always operatic—". . . and many moooore!" As if that wasn't enough, the more socially inept one continues on—"on channel four, and Scooby Doo on channel two, Frankenstein on channel nine"—until, thankfully, someone burns him on the chin with a candle.

○ **The Reminderer.** I love when people try to casually remind people that it's their birthday.

```
            BIRTHDAY BOY
    Man, I can't remember the last
    time my birthday was on a
    Tuesday.


            NEIL
    Hmm? Oh, me neither.


            BIRTHDAY BOY
    It's just that . . .  I only eat
    egg salad on my birthday.
```

Birthday Boy slowly takes a bite of egg salad.
Stares expectantly at Neil.

                    NEIL
         Interesting choice.

                    BIRTHDAY BOY
              (Eyebrows raised, grinning
              expectantly, while nodding
              down to his egg salad)
         Eh?

                    NEIL
         What? . . . Oh! Okay. It's your
         birthday. Okay. I see what you did.

                    BIRTHDAY BOY
         Thanks!

                    NEIL
         For what?

○ **The Extended Birthday.** I think we all know people who
   are never satisfied with a mere day of celebration.
   They like to milk their birthday for at least a week,
   if not longer. You're heading out to dinner with your
   friends, certain that it has something to do with
   your birthday tomorrow, only to find out you're still
   celebrating Melissa's birthday from eight weeks ago.
   I guess the tiara she was wearing should have given
   it away. That, or that ice cream cake she's been toting
   around all night.

High School Reunion Tips

. . . .

1 **Study up on Facebook.** This can be a great tool to re-member names and faces, but be sure to use it wisely. It might appear a tad stalkerish if you start a conversation with a reference to the "Which *Lord of the Rings* Character Are You?" quiz that they took last February. There's really nowhere for the conver-sation to go after this.

2 **Save up.** We had to take out a second mortgage in order to cover our admission cost. I'm still work-ing on the math, but I think it came out to about $35 per drink and $60 per miniature barbecue sandwich.

3 **Use spouse wisely.** If your planners weren't wise enough to provide name tags, use your spouse to find out the names you should already know.[9] Amy and I have the system down to perfection:

---

9. See "Rules for Marriage After Honeymoon Phase Is Over" section on page 155.

```
                    TYLER
               (to classmate)
          There he is!

Double-tap the back of Amy's elbow to initiate
foolproof name investigation system[10]

                    AMY
          Hi, I'm Amy.

                    GUY
          Hi, I'm Neil.

                    TYLER
          Oh, I'm sorry Neil. That was so
          rude of me. I thought you, Neil,
          and Amy had already met. How are
          things in Neil's world . . . Neil?
```

❹ Have phone handy. Any time an awkward silence arises, take out your phone and pretend you have a call. Politely whisper that this is your "new babysitter" as you roll your eyes and apologetically leave the conversation.

❺ Don't talk about old times. Never use the word "remember" to start a sentence. The last thing you want is to be dubbed The Nostalgic Guy who keeps bring-

---

10. One of many marital responsibilities once the honeymoon phase is over. For a complete list, see page 155.

ing up that time you did a group project together sophomore year.

6 **Do talk about old times.** Okay, when Doug gets into his nineteenth consecutive minute of talking about politics, feel free to interject with your favorite thing about that group project sophomore year—even if he wasn't part of the group.

7 **Come with a comfort zone.** Believe it or not, the same cliques exist ten years later. Make sure to bring your clique with you as a comfort zone. Establish a home base early on (near the back), and periodically branch off into the sea of awkwardness, knowing there is a mother ship of social safety that awaits your return.

8 **Chew gum.** Guess who people want to talk to less than Nostalgic Guy? You guessed it—Halitosis Guy.[11] This is your time to display some gum pride[12] and share the love.

9 **Engage in some friendly competition.** Hold a competition among your clique members to see how many different professions you can claim to have throughout the evening. It's amazing how trusting people are.

---

11. Rule of thumb: When someone offers you gum, he's not being nice. He just doesn't want to be in the same room with your current breath.

12. But not too much gum pride (see page 182).

Apparently I can pass for a librarian, a professional scuba diver, a dentist, and a hand model. I'm even scheduled to do a home inspection next Thursday.

⑩ Know when to stay home.   One hundred percent of reunion conversations begin the same way: "What are you up to these days?" If you're nearing thirty and you still don't have a job, it might be best to stay home and play *Madden.* Chances are, you'd rather be doing that anyway, right?

Splitting the Bill

···

can't even enjoy eating with friends anymore. While the rest of them are absorbed in conversation and laughter, I'm stressing out over the upcoming bill split.

                    MY THOUGHTS
          Alright, how is this going to
          work? I ordered the cheese dip,
          but everyone ate it. Is that on
          me? Can you split a cheese dip
          eight ways? What about tip? You
          think she'll include it? I bet
          she will. Dammit—Neil is here. He
          never has enough. He's going to
          ask me to spot him, I just know
          it. Then he'll try to pay me back
          with a partially-used gift card
          or something. Why can't you just
          bring enough cash, Neil? Why are
          you so awful? You do this over,
          and over, and—

                    FRIEND
          —right, Tyler? Wait, are you okay?

                    ME
          What? Me? Yeah . . . I'm cool.

                    FRIEND
          Why are you crying?

Don't Be That Guy: "Get In the Hole" Guy

· ·

There's only one person who is amused when someone yells "get in the hole!" right after a golfer hits the ball[13]—the guy who said it. Everyone else wants to punch him in the throat, ensuring vocal paralysis for the rest of the tournament.

---

13. On his par-5 tee shot, mind you.

An Honest Preflight Video

....

If **we were starting an airline,** this would be our script for the
preflight video:

"Welcome aboard, and thank you for flying with us.
Before we depart, we'd like to go over a few key items
that will help you best experience your flight.

First, be sure to establish your armrest position
early. It's more comfortable to ride in the overhead bin
than to spend two minutes without the armrest. You
didn't pay $300 for this ticket to see how long you can
touch your elbows together.

Your flight is not the time to make friends. If
there's ever a justifiable time to give rude, pithy answers to the person sitting next to you, this is it.
After all, this plane could crash, and you wouldn't
want to spend the last remaining minutes of your
life pretending to care about all the things your seat-
mate did that time he visited the place you're
headed.

NOTE: If the person next to you answers
with single words, doesn't ask you questions in
return, or seems overly interested in an in-flight

magazine article, there's a hint that you're not picking up on.

The answer is always YES when asked if you can fulfill exit row duties. Don't worry. No one has ever paid attention to the exit row responsibilities[14] when being asked to sign off on them. Besides, in the event of an emergency, all of us airline employees will be more concerned with living than grading your door-opening technique.

Just so you know, if someone has to pee, there is no good seat. If you have a window seat, you have to muster up the nerve to wake your sleeping neighbor to go to the bathroom. If you have an aisle seat, you will be woken up no less than six times throughout the duration of your flight so Ol' Micro-Bladder can get his hourly release. There is no win here.

We know you litter in the seatbacks. It's okay. The airplane seatback is one of the only remaining places on earth where it is still acceptable to haphazardly discard wrappers, so go for it. Whenever we come down the aisles with trash bags, just

---

14. I've never been part of an emergency 747 landing, but I imagine touching down in the Gulf of Mexico might cause passengers to abandon proper door-exiting protocol.

remind us that you've got a wastebasket at the end of your knees.

Once we've landed, feel free to stand as soon as the bell dings, even though your head will be at a ninety-degree angle for the next fifteen minutes. You know you look ridiculous, right?

Please—please—preplan your exit. People around you are expecting you to remove your bag from the overhead bin in less than four seconds. There is no room for error here.

This is not the time to put on your jacket. You can endure the microsecond draft you'll feel when crossing the plane-to-jetway threshold. Drape it over your arm and walk like the rest of the passengers.

Again, thank you for flying with us and we hope you tolerate your flight. That's all we can ask."

Real Reasons You're Singing in the Car

· ·

When I'm riding in a car with you and you turn up the volume of the music, I know what you're up to. Without a doubt, it was for one of these seven reasons (in order of frequency):

1 You want to show me that you know all the words to that really fast part of the Barenaked Ladies song.[15]

2 You want to avoid conversation with me.

3 You're showing me that you know how to harmonize.

4 You know where that cool drum part comes in (and what the drummer looks like while doing it).

5 You really like the song but shouldn't,[16] so you want me to think you're blasting it in an ironic way.

---

15. Even though you really started to fade after the "Chickity China the Chinese Chicken" part.

16. See "Party in the USA" by Miley Cyrus.

6 You're trying to get me to ask you who this band is so you can let me know how you're one of the few people who know about them.[17]

7 It's a good song.

All of this is tolerable, but if you start singing along with the guitar solo, please just let me out.

---

17. You'll soon get mad and bail on this band because they "sold out" (aka, "became successful" aka "other people besides you also found out about them and wanted to pay them lots of money to do what they were already doing, but for a much larger audience").

Situations
Involving
Friends

Hug/Handshake Mix-Up

∙∙

Closely akin to the high-five/fist-pound mix-up.

You haven't seen your friend for a while and because of that, you're totally out of sync. The inevitable happens. You go in for the handshake (after all, you're not that great of friends) and he opens wide for the hug (obviously he values your friendship more than you do). Then, like clockwork, both of you switch, only to be in the very same predicament.

We have no advice for this.

Beginner's Guide to Helping Someone Move

•••

I know I'm stating the obvious here, but the real reason any of us help a friend move is so the favor will be returned at some point in the future. That, or he's already helped you and this is your payback. The point is, no one's doing it out of pure kindness. It's too awful.

You will find yourself in this situation sooner or later, though, so you need to be prepared. Here's a guide to help you make this, the most painful of situations, a notch or two less painful.

Timing is everything

You need to approach the unloading of a U-Haul like a game of chess. Always be thinking four to five moves ahead so you don't get stuck carrying the solid oak chest of drawers.

Limp early and often

It is imperative that you make everyone aware[1] that your knee is "flaring up again" so you can avoid hauling a sleeper sofa up two flights of stairs. Speaking of . . .

FACT: Humanity is at its absolute worst when carrying furniture up or down stairs. No one should be held responsible for what they say or how mad they get at inanimate objects.

Don't have an opinion

Any time you get a bunch of guys together to move stuff, each person will have their own opinion about what fits where and what should happen next. Don't waste your breath. The guy who brought his own hand truck and ratchet straps has already thought this through.[2]

Be the guy who hands out boxes

You know who I'm talking about. He's the one who gets up in the truck and just hands stuff out for other people to carry. At first glance, it appears he's taking one for the team. Really, though, he's just taking everyone for a ride.

---

1. Via a group text prior to moving day.

2. Let him have this. He needs it way more than you do.

Moving is like pizza. It's way better with beer.

—Socrates[3]

Three's company, two's a crowd

If there are less than three people involved in the moving process, your friendship will be ruined.[4]

---

3. Kevin Socrates, former neighbor.

4. Your friend knows this. If he has asked you—and only you—to help him move, you're expendable to him. Sorry to break it to you.

Yes, it will all fit

You may think it won't, but it always does. The most powerful thing in the world is the power of not wanting to take two trips.

Or . . . hire movers

Open up a savings account solely dedicated to hiring movers next time someone asks for your help. Best money you'll ever spend.

When You Don't Remember His Name

....

My friend David always talks about his torture chamber idea—it's a room that isn't high enough for you to stand up all the way, but isn't wide enough for you to sit down.

Yeah, that's miserable. But, what about when you're introducing your new friends and you only remember four out of their five names? Is it more miserable than that?

If this has never happened to you, it will. So, here are a few options you have:

1 Say all of their names except for the guy you can't remember, and act as though it was an accident. Then, hopefully, someone will chime in with, "What about John?" At this point laugh innocently and pretend it was an accident.

2 Don't introduce anyone. Simply wait for the other group members to introduce themselves to each other and then apologize for being rude. Trust me, rude is much better than [whatever that trait is where you're too self-absorbed to remember another person's name].

3 Have a celebrity name in your back pocket such as "Barack Obama" that you can use as a joke. I wouldn't advise using my example if the guy you forgot is the only African American standing there.

4 Just pick a random name. Usually you'll get a reaction from your friends like, "Who's that?" Now use the line, "Wait. Wha'd I say?" This way you trick everyone else into figuring out which name you left out.

5 Give the guy you don't remember a cool nickname like, "Ol' Razzle Dazzle" or "Champion Chip" (make sure you wink at him as if he should have known it was coming).

Wrong Name

....

f you're hanging out with a new friend/acquaintance and he calls you the wrong name and you don't correct him, you are now that new name. Period. You had your chance and blew it.[5]

---

5. Tyler: There are currently seven people who know me as "Travis." That's on me.

Manaffection Essentials

ere are some simple instructions for heterosexual men who want to show affection to other heterosexual men.

Hugging

1. Go for the midheight high-five with your right hand, but lean in a little with your shoulder so he knows what's coming.

2. Don't let go, and pull inward. (Your right hands now serve as a buffer eliminating the possibility of a full-torso touch.)

3. With your left hand, reach around behind his back and tap three times. This is code for "I'm not gay."

   Bonus Move: Lean way back during the final release of your initial high-five, and pull as hard as you can with just your fingers. A snapping sound will occur. Sweet!

Kind Words

This one is easy. Just speak from your heart, and then add the word "man" or "dude" (i.e., "I love you, man!" or,

"Dude, this has been fun," or, "I appreciate your advice, man").

Spanking

This is a very delicate move, and it must occur with absolute precision.

❶ First of all, the male-to-male spank can only take place when both parties are dressed for and participating in a team sport. Never attempt when bowling, golfing, fishing, or repairing an engine.

❷ Always spank in public.

❸ Do not make eye contact. In fact, it's better if something else already has your attention before your hand even makes contact.

4 Only spank in a moment of praise. Never spank as a means of discipline.

5 ONLY SPANK ONCE! I cannot overemphasize this.

OKAY: "Nice block, Jim!" [spank] "Let's go, Steve!"

NEVER OKAY: "You can't do that, Mike. That's cheating!" [spank] "Cheating is naughty!" [spank]

Holding hands

This is only okay when saving your friend from falling off of a cliff.

Tickling

Never okay.

Hugging (cont'd)

Now that you know how to properly hug man-to-man, it's important that you understand the appropriate timing. If giving/receiving a bro-hug properly then you should be communicating one of the following messages.

1 **"Great to see you, man. It's been a while."** If you haven't seen each other for quite some time, then go for it. How much time has to go by before the bro-hug is justified? That is up for debate, but one thing is for sure—more than once a week is too much.

❷ **"Farewell, man."** If you are absolutely certain that you won't see each other for a while, a good-bye hug is okay. Just make sure it happens at the last possible second. Say everything you need to say, then hug, then get the hell out of there. There should never be any post-hug conversation. Even avoid eye contact if possible.

❸ **"I'm so sorry."** It's okay to give a comfort hug to another dude who is having a rough time in certain extreme circumstances. Just ask yourself the question, "Did someone die or get dumped?" If your answer is no, you should seriously consider a pat on the shoulder.

❹ **"Thanks, Dad."** Father-son embraces are welcomed and encouraged in most situations: when receiving gifts, after vacations, paid dinner bills, or even when and if he tells you he's proud of you. But, if he's merely refilling your beverage, handing you the remote, or driving you somewhere—no need for an embrace.

❺ **"I'm gay and I hope this progresses."** This pretty much covers every other possible situation.

Rules Regarding Weddings

∙∙

Recently, I was about to send a soon-to-be-married friend the following text: "What on your registry do you need the most in the $30 price range?" It seemed thoughtful and direct, but my wife informed me that this kind of thing is frowned upon. You just don't do it.

Here are a few other essential nuggets to keep in mind the next time a wedding rolls around.

❶ If you haven't been invited, it's never okay to ask the groom where your invitation is. This happened to me. An acquaintance told me point blank that he/she[6] hadn't received the invitation. Naturally, I lied and made up some excuse about how a batch had been returned due to parcel irregularity.

❶b Don't force the groom to make up concepts like parcel irregularity days before his wedding. He has other things to be thinking about.

❷ No one has ever taken an invitation to be an usher as a compliment. It's like the varsity basketball coach letting you sit on the bench with the players,

---

6. And by "he/she," I mean it was a woman around my mom's age. (Don't worry, she'll never read this. She's still mad about the invite.)

but you have to wear khakis and keep track of offensive rebounds on your clipboard.

❸ Grooms: If you haven't used one in the last year, it is not okay to give it as a groomsmen gift.[7] Come on! This is your chance to help us forget about having to drop $175 on a rental tux.

❹ Please let us RSVP via email.

❺ You know when the bride and groom are leaving the reception and everyone lines up and blows bubbles or throws birdseed? Well, I had a random guy drench me with a full glass of water. Just him. Whatever you call that, don't do it.

❻ Grooms: Choose your battles when planning the ceremony. Why would you possibly have an opinion about flower arrangements or groomsmen/bridesmaid pairings? Trust me, there are better hills to die on.

❼ Don't criticize the ceremony. There's a reason the bride and groom didn't consult you when planning it—they don't care what you think. It's their wedding. And besides, they're the only ones who will remember a single detail about it nine minutes after it's over.

❼b Seriously though, bride and groom . . . err on the brief side.

---

7. Money clip, fancy pen, engraved paperweight.

Proper Greeting Etiquette

You may have to double squeeze

Odds are, you're going to run into the Long Squeezer—the guy who likes to shake hands longer than it takes to toast a piece of bread—and you need to have a plan. Do you give a standard squeeze and go limp for the remainder? I say no. I say you go back in with a second squeeze and pretend your temporary limpness was a recurring spasm resulting from early-onset tennis elbow. He'll understand.

Initial greeting = Permanent greeting

Choose it wisely. Nothing is more impossible than trying to work a hug into the mix after years of verbal, no-contact greetings.

Professional athletes and dads are the only ones allowed to engage in custom high-fives. Imagine asking Neil from accounting if he'd like to start one with you.

                    YOU
            (poking head in Neil's office)
        Neil, you got a minute?

                    NEIL
        Sure. Just tying up some loose
        ends on these expense reports.

                    YOU

Well, I was just thinking. We've
been friends for a while now, and
I ... I was just thinking ... I mean,
if it's okay with you, maybe we
could add some steps to our morning
handshake.

                    NEIL

I'm sorry?

                    YOU

I just thought it'd be cool if, when
we shake hands in the mornings,
maybe we could hold on a little
longer at the thumbs and make our
fingers act like butterfly wings. Then
our hands could rise up like the
butterflies are taking them away—

                    NEIL

Um, I don't think—

                    YOU

What? Was it the butterflies?
I mean, I've got other ideas.
There's another one I've been
cooking up that involves a
scissoring motion and a couple
got-your-noses that I think—

                    NEIL

I think I'm getting a phone call.
        (Neil picks up the only thing
        he can find, a banana, and
        holds it to his ear.)

> NEIL (CONT'D)
> Please close the door.

Start the conversation right when you answer the phone

All phones have caller ID now. I know you have my number programmed in, so there really is no need to start the conversation with a 1989 "Hello?" as though you're playing a game of Cell Phone Roulette.[8]

It is possible to bypass greetings altogether

When you see someone nearly every day, a high-five or hug becomes nothing more than an awkward start to your interaction. Like the old adage says, "If it's been a week or two, a hug will do. If it's just been a day, a daily hug will cause the other person to change the route to his destination so that he doesn't have to walk past your cubicle ever again, you sick freak."

---

8. Cell Phone Roulette(™) is a game we came up with that is simultaneously the most fun and most stressful game you'll ever play.

You give your friend your phone. He starts scrolling through your address book until you say stop. He then calls the person he landed on, puts the phone to your ear (without you seeing), and you have to talk with this person until you figure out who it is. You can't ask who it is. You can't say you're playing a game. You must converse as though you just really wanted to catch up.

Just think about how many random numbers you have in your phone—business contacts, college buddies, pest control services. . . . There are so many awful numbers it could land on.

You're welcome.

5 Levels of Greeting Intimacy

● **The Neck Snap.** This is a quick, aggressive look away after you've accidentally made eye contact. Use this when you see old or annoying acquaintances who you'd rather not have a conversation with, such as that guy you sat next to in high school Biology who was entirely too enthusiastic about all the human anatomy diagrams.

❷ **The Head Nod.** You can go one of two ways here: The Upper or the Downer. The Upper (accompanied by an exaggerated eyebrow lift) says, "What's up?" but eliminates the need for actual conversation. The Downer (accompanied by a minor frown and tucking of chin into the neck) tells the recipient that you're glad to have crossed paths and that you approve of his shirt choice.

❸ **The Handshake.** There's nothing more important than a good handshake. If someone pulls a quick-grab[9] though, immediately call for a do-over. A

---

9. You know the quick-grab. He squeezes too early, grabbing only your fingers, causing you to curl your hand upward, as though he is about to kiss it and you feel the need to curtsy.

little bit of awkwardness here is better than letting him go through the day thinking those thoughts about you.

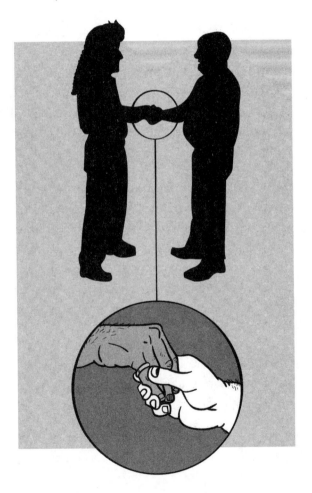

4 **The Five-and-a-Half.** This is a right-handed sideways five with a left-arm wraparound half-hug. Never switch sides on this. If you do, you will confuse your partner and end up giving each other a three and wrapping around into each other's face. Oh, and never try this with a female. There are just too many ways it could go wrong.

5 **The Embrace.** Once you've reached hugging status, use them wisely. They are only appropriate as bookends to your encounter—once at the greeting, and once at the closing. Using them between the bookends, such as when your friend gets back from the bathroom or before you get in the car together, will jeopardize your relationship and take you back to head-nod status.

Things Guys Never Do with or Around Other Guys

❍ Drop off at the door of a restaurant if it's raining.

❍ Use emoji in a text.

❍ Use the words "cute" or "awwww."

❍ Apply sunscreen to another man anywhere other than his back.

"Can you, um . . . get my back?"

○ Make eye contact while complimenting one another.

○ Share a toothbrush.

○ Check each other's breath.

○ Give each other a haircut at the same time.

○ Stay together while shopping in a department store.

○ Share a smaller-than-king-sized bed.

○ Not overreact to an accidental hand brush while walking side-by-side.

○ Admit when your feelings have been hurt.

○ Hold in a fart.

Quit Making Me Try Something

....

> Two men sit together at a
> table.

>   GUY
> Dude, this is amazing.

>   TRIPP
> Oh yeah? Mine's pretty good, too.

>   GUY
> No, this is unbelievable. Wanna
> try it?

>   TRIPP
> Nah, I'm fine.

>   GUY
> You gotta try this. You're going
> to love it.

>   TRIPP
> I don't really like seafood.

>   GUY
> You'll like this. It tastes like
> steak.

Realizing logic is out the window, Tripp relents.

>   TRIPP
> Ok.

Tripp takes a bite.

Guy stares in anticipation as Tripp chews.

He smiles big.

Tripp is almost done chewing.

Guy starts to nod a little.

>   GUY
>   It's amazing isn't it?

>   TRIPP'S THOUGHTS
>   It's actually pretty good. Nothing
>   to get excited about, but that's
>   just it. I know he wants nothing
>   less than full-on enthusiasm.

>   TRIPP
>   Yeah, it's really good.

>   GUY
>   I know right? So good. Isn't it
>   like the best thing you've ever
>   tasted?

>   TRIPP
>   (swallowing)
>   That was really good.

Maybe your thing isn't food. Maybe it's a new band we just have to hear or your insistence that we go way out of the way for this new restaurant we just have to try. Regardless, we're never going to be as excited as you are about it. Please remember this.

Being Partially Paid Back

....

Bro, either pay me back or don't. If you owe me $20, don't you dare give me a ten-spot and tell me the other half is "on the way." I'd rather you had just kept your $10 and avoided me for the next two years.

Oh, and paying me back with a mix CD[10] is unacceptable.

---

10. Unless the mix CD is perfectly made by using the following formula:

Happy and energetic song
  "Semi-Charmed Life" by Third Eye Blind

Song I love but forgot about
  "Crossroads" by Bone Thugs-N-Harmony

Awesome song that I will skip
  "Mambo No. 5" by Lou Bega

Obscure song that only has meaning to you and me
  "Marianne" by Matt Wertz

Song I can show-off-lip-sync to
  "One Week" by Barenaked Ladies

Slow song that makes me feel good even though the words are stupid
  "Damn Cold Night" by Avril Lavigne

Something you sneak in hoping I'll like and then credit you for introducing me to
  "Sneaky Tuesday" by the Uptown Suicidal's

The perfect song
  "Interstate Love Song" by Stone Temple Pilots

You Don't Need to Justify Your Purchases

••

The Financial Analyst

This person likes to explain the financial logic behind seemingly extravagant purchases, just to make sure everyone knows how reasonable and legitimate they are. They're so reasonable, in fact, that he'd have been foolish to have abstained.

> NEIL
> Nice jeans! How much did those set you back?

> FINANCIAL ANALYST
> Um, a lot.

> NEIL
> Like, $100?

> FINANCIAL ANALYST
> Yeah, basically . . . $100 . . . $169. Somewhere around there.

> NEIL
> You paid over $150 for jeans?

> FINANCIAL ANALYST
> Look, I don't wear suits to work, I wear jeans. And considering

```
these jeans cost less than half
of what you'd pay for a good suit,
I'm actually being thrifty.

            NEIL
Hmm. Not sure you know what
thrifty means.
```

The Storyteller

This person likes to spin elaborate yarns about the lore behind the actual purchase. When encountering a storyteller I feel like exclaiming, "Look, guy, I was just making small talk. I had no idea my 'That's a nice TV' comment was going to elicit a purchase testimony that included an inciting incident, flashbacks for character development, and an intermission for refreshments. Instead of telling me it was the deal of the century because it was the display model and that you talked the guy down another $200 and that this off-brand is actually made by the same company that makes the on-brand, we could actually be watching it right now."

The Thank You Replacer

This person doesn't waste any time with pleasantries. Her primary purpose in every conversation is to let the other person know she avoided paying retail price.

SHEILA
Hey, nice scarf!

TYR
Target. Eight eighty-nine.

SHEILA
Um, okay. I really like those
jeans, too. Are those—

TYR
Seventeen dollars. eBay.

SHEILA
Wow, you . . . have a great
memory.

TYR
Brain Age for Nintendo DS . . .
nineteen dollars at GameStop.

SHEILA
Um . . . You're . . . welcome?

Advice That Needs to Go

....

○ **"Just think about where you saw it last."** Is this necessary advice? When you lose something, it's impossible not to immediately think about where you had it last. If you could picture where you had it last, you wouldn't be having this conversation.

○ **And please don't tell me to retrace my steps.** Can we just forever assume that every person who has lost something has already exhausted both of these options?

Situations Involving (More Than) Friends

Ruining Valentine's Day
(How to Get Dumped)

If you're in a relationship that you want to last, please refrain from getting your significant other any of the following items:

A playlist

There was something so raw and romantic about a mix tape or CD—the manual labor involved, the title you chose, the blank tape/CD brand choice, the personalized cover art. There's something about dragging a few songs over to the iTunes sidebar and syncing up her iPod when she isn't looking that doesn't really have the same effect.

Hand-me-down electronics

Getting her an iPhone 5 = awesome. Giving her your old iPhone 5 as a gift because you just upgraded to the superior iPhone 5S = not awesome.

A homemade coupon book

"One free back rub." Really? Have you been charging for the other ones? If you haven't learned it already, your wife will receive a back rub from you whenever she pleases.

Store credit

Giving her a gift card is bad enough. But giving her a $26.17 Lowe's merchandise credit card that you received when you took back that extra weather stripping is completely unacceptable.

Postponement

There's a 0 percent chance she's going to fall for the ol' "I was thinking we could celebrate Valentine's Day on the 16th this year" routine. You aren't edgy and eccentric. You forgot . . . and she knows it.

A future experience with no documentation

Nothing says "I forgot to get you something, but managed to come up with a great idea on the way downstairs" like the future shared experience with no documentation (or FSEWND). A concert with no tickets, a day at the spa with no reservation, a night away without the hotel confirmation . . . they're not going to happen. Trust me on this.

A future experience with documentation

Nothing says "I forgot to get you something, but managed to come up with a great idea and printed it out just before I came downstairs" like the ol' future shared experience with documentation (or FSEWD).[1]

---

1. I guess what we're trying to say is your gift shouldn't involve a printout.

Nothing

Apparently, in the context of Valentine's Day, "let's not get each other anything this year" doesn't actually mean "let's not get each other anything this year." It means "At the very least, something small and thoughtful. But for the love of everything holy, not nothing. Nothing would be the single worst thing you could do. Never do nothing."

Rules for Marriage After Honeymoon Phase Is Over

....

○ When at a party together, wife must discreetly find out the name of the guy the husband is supposed to know and is currently trapped in a conversation with.

○ Wife gets to occupy nine out of ten bathroom drawers and monopolize closet space.

○ Wife shall determine the temperature of the house. Husband is not to adjust said temperature by one degree, even if one of the reasons he works so hard is so he can be comfortable in his own house.

○ Husband must find out hard way that shower curtains are supposed to be cleaned.

○ Sheets shall be washed eight times more frequently than husband was accustomed to prior to marriage. Also, husband's former sheets are to be burned.

○ Wife's fingernails are to double as husband's makeshift dental floss when his multiple attempts have failed and they're about to walk into a restaurant.

○ Wife is to never bring up the time Husband sharted[2] in the car on the way to dinner with friends.

○ Wife must regularly shave husband's neck and remove his stray back hairs whenever they sprout, especially before a beach vacation.

○ Husband's honest opinion of dinner shall remain suppressed until at least twenty-four hours after wife has asked.

○ Wife shall not make eye contact with husband during the "Move That Bus" segment of *Extreme Makeover: Home Edition* in case husband was affected in a way he wasn't expecting.

---

2. Google it (but make sure it's not a Google Image search).

A Step-by-Step Guide to Surviving Chick Flicks

....

Chick flicks (aka Rom-coms, aka anything with Kate Hudson in it) are inevitable in relationships. It's crucial that men know how to properly handle themselves in these situations.

Just follow these eleven simple steps any time your wife/girlfriend chooses the movie.

1 Passive-aggressively scoff at her initial chick-flick suggestion. Don't overdo it, but make it loud enough to demonstrate your boundless masculinity to other males within earshot.

2 Roll eyes during previews for good measure. Sighs are optional.

3 After his first shirtless scene, whisper disturbing information about chiseled male protagonist you learned during an "accidental" TMZ viewing prior to the movie.

4 Suppress sudden twinge of emotion that you just felt.

5. Insist to wife that you don't understand how people find the lead actress attractive and that you cannot fathom why her face has been chosen to grace the cover of numerous magazines.

6. Forego urge to use the restroom, despite drinking the equivalent of a twelve-pack of Fanta Orange in the last half hour, so you don't miss what Kate Hudson says when the love interest says what he said he was going to say.

7. Feel another twinge of emotion, this time accompanied by mild eye-moistening. Rub temples with index finger of hand-shield and cough to hide your true feelings from everyone who is now watching you instead of the movie.

8. Ride home in silence.

9. Once wife is asleep, succumb to your sudden impulse to journal about the paradox of love—its complexity, its simplicity, and your thankfulness that Hugh Grant has taught you how seamlessly they can be woven together.[3]

---

3. This may or may not be an actual excerpt from a journal entry, circa the time *Notting Hill* was in theaters.

⑩ Deny having seen said movie when friends and co-workers talk about it. Quickly change the subject by spouting off obscure facts about Ben Savage[4] you researched on IMDb for just such an occasion.

⑪ Repeat.

---

4. Did you know he played the same character, Cory Matthews, in *Boy Meets World* (1993), *Teen Angel* (1997), and *Maybe This Time* (1995)?

How to Know If Your Boyfriend Is Insecure

....

Here are thirteen surefire ways to tell if a man is insecure (sorry for letting the cat out of the bag, guys):

1 Is he constantly implementing the touch flex? You know the touch flex—when you grab his arm in the bicep/tricep region, triggering an immediate flex in an attempt to show you that his arm is always like that. Try asking him a question. Nothing. He's holding his breath for maximum results.

2 Does he adamantly declare "I'm off today" when underperforming in sports? He just wants to make sure you know that this is not how it normally goes down. He normally makes zero mistakes and is perfect.

3 Does he constantly disclose how sore he is? We've all been there. He joins the conversation with a loud, uncomfortable sigh, and you have no choice but to ask him what's wrong. He'll spend the next ten minutes giving you a play-by-play of his last three bench sets and how sore they have made him.

❹ Can he steer any conversation back to his glory days?

> CO-WORKER
> Did you get that memo I faxed you yesterday?

> INSECURE GUY
> Wow. That is crazy.

> CO-WORKER
> What? It was about our new accounting policy.

> INSECURE GUY
> No . . . wow. The way you said that . . .

> CO-WORKER
> (confused)

> INSECURE GUY
> . . . it's just . . . you sounded just like that home plate umpire after I hit that game-winning dinger.

> CO-WORKER
> Ok . . . great job. About that fa—

> INSECURE GUY
> It was against Central. We took region that night. Anyway, what were you saying?

5 Is he wearing his fraternity T-shirt right now?
This is the young professional version of wearing
your high school letter jacket in college. Bro, it's
time. Take it off, put it in a trash bag, and take it to
Goodwill.

6 Does he go to the tanning bed to get a "base tan"?
Don't believe what he tells you. He's not worried
about getting sunburned. He's worried about not
looking fantastic when he takes his shirt off.

7 Are his biceps bigger than his thighs? I wonder
what this guy does at the gym? Cardio? A full-body

routine? No. This guy's paying $30/month in membership fees to use a curl bar.

8 Does he take full advantage of handshakes? This is his time to make sure you know he is stronger than you. In the facial region, he's all smiles. Down in the hand region, he's attempting to grind your knuckles into a fine bone powder.

9 Does he downsize in the shirt department? He should be wearing an XL, but instead opts for a Medium. This ensures him minimum range of motion, but maximum display of muscle. The goal here is for it to seem like he has no shirt on at all.

10 Does he smell too good? Listen, guy. It's okay to smell bad at the gym. Everyone there expects you to smell exactly like they do.

11 Is he really proud of his car's sound system? If he hasn't told you about it six times already, it's okay. If you're within a three-mile radius of his car while he's driving, you'll know all you need to know.

12 Does he know more about football than Chris Mortensen? No one should know more about football than Mort. This guy loves sliding random football tidbits into any all-male conversation, marking his territory so to speak. He wants everyone to know that he's the go-to guy if a debate arises over the details of Darrelle Revis's new contract or who played in the 1995 AFC Championship game.

⓭ Did he publish a book that makes fun of various types of people? This is the deepest form of insecurity. There is no hope for these men.

Situations Involving Certain Other People

Open Letter to People without Kids

Dear people without kids,

Hello! I hope you've been enjoying doing whatever the hell you want, whenever the hell you want to, and not taking for granted the massive amount of freedom you have that makes all people with kids hate you.

Right this second, you are at your most idealistic about parenting. You've read all the books, taken all the classes, and discussed all of the popular parenting philosophies. Little do you know, you'll forget all about your promise to "never shove candy in your kid's face to get him to shut up" the first time your baby decides to freak out in an airplane. I know. I was you.

You close the door too loud. It's a proven fact that, when a kid is sleeping, the single loudest thing in a house is a door latching shut. From now on, twist the knob, open, walk through, twist the knob again, and release at the exact point the latch lines up with the hole. If it makes it easier, pretend you're a spy or something.

The current TV volume is what we have chosen to be the maximum acceptable volume. When our kids are sleeping, take our subtle hints. We've chosen volume level 27 for a reason. We're whispering to each other for a reason. We're "calling it a night" and escorting you to the door for a reason.

Don't parent my kids. If I haven't put a stop to what my kid is doing, you shouldn't feel the need to. Chances are, he's probably used to doing that thing because the people who created him have previously approved of it.

Men, it is never okay to touch a pregnant woman's stomach without an invitation. I don't go around touching your wife's abs just because I heard she's been working out, do I? Same thing (I'm told).

When a baby is freaking out in public, feel sorry for the parents. Sure, your natural tendency is to get mad at the infant for acting like . . . an infant. But let me challenge you to redirect that anger into something more worthwhile—sympathy for the parents. Trust me, they're the ones in pain.

Thanks for your time. Enjoy the movie theater!

Tyler

General Problems with Weathermen

○ Ten-day forecast, huh? Seeing as how you were wrong about this afternoon's scattered showers when you reported it this morning, where do you get off telling us what will happen two Tuesdays from now? Maybe settle down on the extended forecast and get tonight's prediction right, Tony Thunderclap.

○ Don't tell me about hot air masses colliding with cold air masses. I don't need a meteorology lesson. I just need to know if I should be wearing a football helmet indoors.

○ Here are a few things you don't need to include in any weather report: barometric pressure, other states' weather, actual pollen count, or fronts of any kind.

○ Easy on the graphics. I know technology has come a long way, but once graphics overtake land on the map, you should consider toning it down.

○ Those of us who live outside the Midwest can never remember the difference between a "tornado warning" and a "tornado watch." One I can play tag with my kids in the yard. One has my family of five sleeping in a bathtub.

○ Don't act excited. I know this storm is creating a high-pressure system in the crotchal region of your pants right now, but people are in danger.

○ And for the love, have a clue about the shape of the storm you are talking about and the motions you choose to describe it, lest the forecast turn into an X-rated production. How many penis-shaped storms can there really be?

Computer Tips for Mom and Dad

○ You don't have to double-click web links.

○ You have other email address options[1] than the one issued to you by your Internet provider. Nothing says "Greatest Generation" quite like "[your name]1949@bellsouth.net."

○ You don't have to shut down your computer after every use.

○ You probably don't need four different free-trial antivirus programs running simultaneously on your computer.

○ You don't need to act overly ignorant about social media. So you're not a user. That's fine. But when one out of every five people in the world with computer access is a member, there is absolutely no excuse for you to still call it "FaceSpace," "Spacebook," or "MyFace."

○ Your text doesn't need a salutation.

---

1. Oh, and is an audible voice still letting you know that you've got mail when you "log on"? If so, might be time to move digital mailboxes.

○ You don't need to type in "http://www." anymore. In the time it's taking you to find those forward slashes, I could have visited the site, restarted my computer, made a sandwich, eaten the sandwich, and upgraded my computer's firmware.

○ You should consider Googling something first. Google knows every answer to every question ever conceived. Google is never busy. And Google is never going to judge you for asking a stupid question. Search first, ask last.[2]

---

2. While it's true that this will eventually lead to humanity's descent into crippling stupidity, sometimes there's just no time to wonder who the guy is that plays opposite Zack Morris on that TNT lawyer show (Answer: Breckin Meyer. Score another one for Google.)

Don't Be That Guy: Screen Toucher

....

Hey, **guy** who really wants to show us something on the computer. Instead of stabbing my screen with your index finger with a force that could pierce skin, resulting in a permanent rainbow-colored bruise on the center of my screen that will last until the end of time, try pointing next time. I think you'll be surprised by its effectiveness.

"Send that file on over to me. The one right . . . there."

Guy with a Pre-Dice Roll Ritual

f I have to spend one more second watching you blow on the dice or shake them vigorously for eight seconds prior to your roll, I might just stab myself with this mini-pencil I'm using to keep score.

I'm not sure which is more absurd—the ritual itself, the fact that you actually believe your ritual works, or the fact that I'm using a mini-pencil.

Open Letter to My Dental Hygienist

....

Dear Dental Hygienist,

I'm really grateful for what you do, but I have eight small requests . . .

Please refrain from carving your initials into my gums. I happened to catch a glimpse of my mouth after you finished attacking me with your metal scraper and it looked like I'd been gnawing on a ketchup packet for the past hour.

Please keep your disapproving "mmh"s to yourself. Even though I'm a whole two feet away from you, I can still hear your audible condemnation, and I feel like I'm about to be grounded.

Please stop showing me X-rays. I really appreciate the gesture, but I have no clue what I'm looking at. Trying to locate that cavity you're pointing out makes me feel a little like I'm staring at a Magic Eye poster trying to see a 3-D centaur.

Please eat something before my appointment. Nothing has ever been closer to your stomach than my ear. You were either starving, holding back a fart, or two of your organs were mating inside of you. Whichever one it was, I no longer feel comfortable making eye contact with you.

"Mhmm, mhmm, mhmm . . . I'm gonna take your word for it."

Please use discretion when asking an open-ended question. When I have a mouth wedge, two impression trays, and four utensils crammed into my mouth, it's probably not the best time to ask me what my weekend plans are.

Please use some of the money I pay you on modern toothbrushes. Anything but what I can only assume is the original toothbrush.[3] I need lots of aerodynamics and bristles going in at least eight different directions. Oh, and if it's not two-toned, just put it in the trash can and skip the middleman.

---

3. You know, the flat, solid-color, ninety-degree bristled piece of garbage that you can't even purchase anymore; you can only "win" at a Chuck E. Cheese's ticket redemption counter.

Please tell me if I need to clean my face off. I love getting back in the car after a long conversation with the receptionist, only to look in the rearview mirror and see plaque nuggets all over my cheeks. And all this time I thought she was laughing at my sharp wit.

Please forgive me in advance for failing to change. Every time it's the same old song and dance. I leave you with an incredibly strong resolve to change. I'll floss divots in my gums for the next three days, but I promise you, it won't last. If you can't handle this, we might need to start seeing other people.

If you could just get those eight things worked out, I (and the rest of humanity) would really appreciate it. Thanks!

Sincerely,
Tripp and Tyler

Don't Be That Guy:
Expert Poker Player

....

'm not bothered by the fact that he is good. I'm bothered by the fact he wants everyone to know how good he is.

You know the guy. He's the one who makes sure you know he can shuffle better than you. He's proud of how fast he can deal. He's the first guy to point out that a straight beats a three-of-a-kind and he's hell-bent on fitting all the poker lingo he knows into table conversation.

And he is the main reason I don't play poker.

Don't Be That Guy: Grammar Nazi

●●

know you were probably expecting a slow-motion celebratory embrace when you interrupted my story to inform me I should have said "me" instead of "I," but that won't be happening any time soon. Or ever.

All my energy is going toward figuring out if it is possible for you and I[4] to never be in a conversation again.

---

4. I know—should have been "me." Just trying to piss off the Grammar Nazi.

I Already Know Everything About You . . .

....

○ . . . if you excessively decorate your front yard for all major holidays.

○ . . . if your phone has ever been in a belt clip and that belt clip has ever been on your belt.

○ . . . if your favorite movie stars the Wayans brothers.

○ . . . if you wear your Bluetooth device outside your car.

○ . . . if you're still using AOL.

○ . . . if you've impersonated Ace Ventura in the last week.

○ . . . if you have a tattoo higher than the collar of your shirt.

○ . . . if you and your spouse wear matching shirts.

○ . . . if you refer to coffee as "java," pizza as "za," or dollars as "bones."

○ . . . if there's a toothpick in your mouth right now.

○ ... if you express your political viewpoints via bumper stickers.

○ ... if your tip ever includes pennies.

○ ... if you give people massages without them asking.

○ ... if you wear athletic jerseys while not participating in athletics.

○ ... if you've peeled out on purpose in the last forty-eight hours.

○ ... if you spend more than $100 on sunglasses or headphones.

○ . . . if you give me grilling tips while I'm grilling.

"You gonna move that one away from the flame?"

○ . . . if you do squats and you're not in high school.

○ . . . if you've ever shown someone your abs.

○ . . . if you can name more *Real Housewives* cast members than U.S. Congressmen.

○ . . . if you've tried to convince me why I should invest in gold.

○ . . . if I smell like you after we hug.

Don't Be That Gum Chewer

The Aggressor

Gum is part of this guy's image. No one is left wondering whether or not he is chewing it either. He makes sure his lips never touch and that his jaw continues in a violent counterclockwise motion. He chews so aggressively that you wonder if he's gnawing on a Lego tire. You'll find him in the center of a room with his head on a swivel to make sure people from all angles can admire him.

The Popper

This person doesn't want to leave any room to guess whether or not she is chewing gum. She constantly pops it, as if to say, "Just wanted to make sure all of you in the Tri-State Area knew I was enjoying some gum."

The Evangelist

This guy audibly scoffs when you pull out your brand of choice. When he asks you if you've tried his brand, he's not actually offering you a piece. He is simply making a statement about his superior lot in life. He feels sad that you haven't graduated from Cinnaburst and experienced the riches of the Orbitz cubes that he ritually swears by.

The Halfer

I know the economy is bad, but is it really time to start rationing your gum? No one likes half a piece.[5] It feels like a sliver of food that you had stuck in your teeth has finally come loose and is floating around in your mouth. Personally, I'd rather just stick with my bad breath.

The Dealer

This person never comes out and asks if you'd like a piece of gum. He always treats the exchange like a drug deal,

---

5. Especially when you've chosen to half the piece with your front teeth. I know, you worked hard not to touch it with your lips, but I can't help but feel like there's still some plaque transfer taking place.

like he's smuggled in some illegal pills from Nepal or something. He comes up real close to you and pulls the pack halfway out of his pocket, looks at it, then looks at you. He doesn't say a word; he just lifts his eyebrows a little. He's afraid that if any words are exchanged his cover will be blown and the contraband will be confiscated.

Christmas Gifts for an Enemy

∙∙

Christmas is a hectic time of organizing parties, family get-togethers, and of course scrambling around malls and/or the Internet for gifts. News segments, magazine articles, and coffeehouse conversations all around the world are devoting serious time and energy to finding that special gift for that special someone in your life.

What about your enemies though? Don't they deserve that kind of thought? Don't they have feelings, too? I mean, sure . . . they're expecting a terrible gift. But the least you could do is make it a terrible gift from the heart. After all, it is the thought that counts.

Here's a list of what I'm getting my enemies:

○ A Ke$ha CD inside a Mumford & Sons jewel case

○ Entire season of *Lost* on VHS

○ A used Dental-Floss-Scented candle

○ A two-year Boost Mobile contract (with free flip phone)

○ Front-row seats at a Nickelback concert (with Creed opening)

○ A Hallmark card with nothing inside

○ Three pairs of my old carpenter jeans

○ A *World Book Encyclopedia* set

○ A bar of soap and washcloth[6]

○ The task of returning an item to Target

○ Twelve pounds of black licorice

○ A guilt trip

○ A 26.6k modem

○ My passport photo, blown up and framed

○ The process of buying and selling a used car

○ The responsibility of faxing something for me

○ A conversation about politics

○ A post-kitten-aged cat that still has many years left to live

○ A *Caillou* box set for their kids to watch on a long car ride

○ A pamphlet of any kind

○ A Zune with no gift receipt[7]

---

6. With pubic hair embedded deeply in both.

7. We realize you would probably have laughed a lot harder at this joke in 2007.

Don't Be That Guy:
Sports Fan

....

The Homer

His team has never done wrong. Every penalty, bad play, and loss will somehow be blamed on poor officiating. Simple correlation: The greater the Homer, the less tolerable he is to watch sports with.

The Fighter

I was at a game once where two guys started getting into a verbal sparring match. They eventually got to a point where fighting was the next logical step. Guy #1 shouted, "You wanna take this outside?!" Guy #2 exclaimed, "We are outside!" Then the hundred fans surrounding them mocked Guy #1 until he sat down in shame. Best fight I've ever seen.[8][9]

The Pessimist

This is the perfect way to describe us Georgia Tech fans. When something bad happens, we curse the team and

---

8. True story.

9. Don't you hate it when someone says "True story" when the story is incredibly believable?

shout things like "Classic Tech!" When something good happens, we act overly surprised (especially in a crowd of people) and shout derisive things like, "Don't worry . . . give 'em a second . . . THERE's the fumble!" While depressing, this mind-set is effective at preventing true disappointment.

The Authority

This guy begins 88 percent of his sentences with the phrase "I'll tell you what happened . . . " followed by some regurgitated viewpoint that he heard Mike and Mike[10] make on the radio that morning.

The Wave Starter

When I was fifteen, I started[11] a 50,000-person "Beat L.A." chant at an Atlanta Braves game. There isn't a greater feeling in life, knowing that you single-handedly birthed a 1.5-minute revolution. This is precisely why The Wave Starter exists. He's tasted the magic and wants nothing more than another shot at glory.

You know the guy I'm talking about. He had thirteen Natty Lights during the pregame tailgate. He proudly dons a T-shirt from a sorority function he went to back in

---

10. Or [insert favorite dogmatic sports talk personality].

11. Some may challenge this assertion.

'01 and wears sunglasses with Croakies (even though it's a night game). Oh, and he's always ready to fight.

He'll devote no less than four innings to making this wave happen. Eight minutes in, he's sweatier than any of the players on the field. You think about joining in, but decide against it. Now he's pissed at you. He keeps telling you to Come on! and you do your best to act interested in

"C'mon! For real this time, you guys! Here we go . . ."

the program's cover article. At some point, the game on the field is no longer important to you. All you care about is defeating The Wave Starter and crushing his dreams.

Eventually, the crowd will give in. The wave will make a victorious half-lap before dying out in left-center field. The Wave Starter will tell this heroic tale for the next five decades—how he overcame the odds, defeated the villain (you), and brought dozens to their feet.

Situations We Wanted to Include in the Book but Couldn't Figure Out How to Categorize

Laughter Accessories

For some people, a standard laugh just isn't getting the job done. You know the people I'm talking about. Chances are you know one of these people . . . or are one.

- ○ **The Toucher.** This person feels the need to pepper his laughter with some sort of physical contact . . . anything from a forearm caress to a full-on bicep grab.

- ○ **The Praiser.** This person isn't satisfied with merely laughing at every joke ever told. No, he wants to make sure you know that your joke was the one. His levels of endorsement range from high-fives and fist pounds to reverent post-laugh commentary.

- ○ **The Whiplasher.** He violently snaps his head backwards as though his car has just been rear-ended.

- ○ **The Verbalizer.** Someone delivers a joke, and instead of trying to muster up an audible laugh, he goes straight into a complimentary statement: "Bro, that is hilarious."

- ○ **The Sprinkler.** Once the clever one-liner is delivered, this person goes wide-mouth and pans across the room, bouncing from person to person, before whipping back to the original jokester.

○ **The Wind-Downer.** He tries to wrap up his laughter, but keeps going back into it.

○ **The Doesn't Get It-er.** You'll be able to identify this guy by how much he looks around the room while fake laughing.

○ **The Explainer.** He's annoying to everyone except The Doesn't Get It-er.

○ **The Mimer.** It's amazing how wide this person's mouth can be open, how much his shoulders can bounce, and how tightly he can close his eyes without registering a single decibel.

○ **The Repeater.** This person somehow manages to repeat the punchline and sometimes the entire joke while laughing.

Women, Please Stop . . .

○ Calling each other "chica."

○ Providing high ratings to terrible TV programming.

○ Saying "I need to lose weight" in front of other women who are clearly fatter than you.

○ Blaming the entire male race for the way you've been treated by a few jerks (who you chose to date).

○ Getting upset when we disparage women's basketball.[1]

○ Acknowledging that you fart—I shouldn't even have to tell you this.

---

1. A well-timed WNBA joke is always funny.

Men, Please Stop . . .

○ Calling each other "broseph."[2]

○ Subtly putting shirtless photos of yourself onto Facebook.

○ Adding racing stripes, ground effects, subwoofers, lifts, or tailpipes to your car.

○ Wearing sunglasses indoors.

---

2. Unless it's your brother named Joseph, then by all means.

Pretentiousness

My computer's built-in dictionary defines pretentiousness as "attempting to impress by affecting greater importance, talent, culture, etc., than is actually possessed."

If any of the following describes you, your friends are probably describing you as pretentious behind your back.

Saying a band "sold out"

I remember saying this about John Mayer a few years ago. I took great pleasure in letting people know I listened to him back when he was playing an acoustic guitar and singing ballads about his stupid mouth. I couldn't believe he would want to get paid millions of dollars more to do what he was already doing for a much larger audience.[3]

Scoffing at light beer

I completely understand that different people have different preferences in the beer aisle. But acting as though drinking a light beer would permanently scar your esophageal tract and send you into a mild depression is a bit overdramatic. True, it's not your usual double IPA. But it's also not cat urine.

---

3. Now I can. I hope I get to sell out one day.

Watching English Premiere League Soccer

When you set your alarm to 4 am so you can watch the quarterfinal match between Leeds United and Aston Villa, are you doing it because you really love it, or because you really love telling people you love it?

Putting an Apple sticker on your car

You're just letting the PC world know you're better at life than they are. We really can't argue with you.

Saying the movie wasn't as good as the book

My first experience in this department was with John Grisham's *The Firm*. The only problem was that I couldn't find anyone who had seen the movie to brag to. So I did what anyone else in my situation would have done. I tried to slide it into a conversation about Derek Jeter. They may not have acted like it, but deep down I think they were impressed.

Only listening to records

Call me whatever the opposite of old-fashioned is, but is the sound really as good as you swear it is? I mean, I'm open to being wrong here, but am I really supposed to prefer the consistent crackle of a record?

Using the word "tannins"

Look, just because you used your wine-tasting Groupon last weekend doesn't mean you are now qualified to start talking like a sommelier.

Swearing art is objective

Every now and then I'll vocalize my dislike of a particular piece of art—be it a song or painting or movie—and will be promptly told that I just "don't understand." That if I just "understood" a little more, I'd appreciate it. Listen, pal. That's not how art works. Nothing you say is going to make me impressed with the *Mona Lisa.* And as much as it pains me to say it, nothing I say is going to make you impressed with *The Wire.*[4]

Calling movies "films"

A subtle move, yes. But we know that, inside, you are screaming for someone to notice.

Finding it hard to believe someone doesn't have an iPhone

When a friend tells me he doesn't have an iPhone, I immediately assume they were sold out when he went to buy one or that he did have one and then tragically lost it

---

4. You really should watch it. Objectively speaking, it's the *Mona Lisa* of TV shows.

somehow. Something along those lines. Never, though . . . never do I assume it's because he just didn't want one. You know what? Screw what I said earlier. There is one piece of art that is objectively good—the iPhone.

Signs of a TV Addict

1 As a kid, was the most exciting part of your summer vacation the ability to watch *The Price is Right*?

2 Would you literally give anything for a TV in the bathroom?

3 When you're having a heart-to-heart with your child, do you require your spouse to play *Full House*-esque music softly in the background?

4 Can you sing the entire *Mr. Belvedere* opening song[5] right now?

5 Do you judge people who judge people for watching too much TV?

6 When you ask people about their favorite shows, are you secretly looking for an enabler?

7 Do you wish, not that there were more hours in a day, but that there were more hours of *Law & Order: SVU* in a day?

---

5. Just found out it's "streaks on the China," not "straight from-a China." This makes much more sense than rationalizing Mr. Belvedere being an immigrant from Shanghai.

The Netflix "Just One . . . More . . . Episode" Side Glance

8 Did you petition to name your first child Dwayne Wayne?

9 When your wife objected, did you suggest Doogie, saying that it would significantly increase his chances of becoming a child prodigy?

10 Has your favorite song ever been a commercial jingle?

11 Have you ever referred to watching *Mad Men* as "getting a fix"?

⑫ Have you ever planned a family vacation around your favorite shows?

⑬ Do you still recognize and celebrate *TGIF*?

⑭ Did you cry when you found out your grandparents didn't have TV growing up?

⑮ Have you ever given your wife a carefully crafted presentation on why you need a sixty-inch flat-screen?

⑯ Do you take someone's cable package into consideration before starting a friendship?

⑰ Have you ever referred to Comcast as your "dealer?"

⑱ Are you concerned that your kid's homework is going to interfere with his TV schedule?

AP Driver's Ed

....

believe Driver's Ed has fallen woefully short in helping today's drivers excel behind the wheel.

Sure, you'll learn your share of moderately important
information, but I believe they've missed the overarch-
ing point of what the Driver's Ed experience should be.
They've presented driving to us as a task, a mere means
of transport, as opposed to what it truly is—an art form.

Thus, we present to you AP Driver's Ed, guaranteed to
enrich your experience behind the wheel as well as the
experiences of those around you.

The Pre-Wave

This is one of the most essential tools in the tool belt of
any driver. What is a pre-wave, exactly? With a mere raise
of the hand, you essentially thank a person in advance
for letting you cut him off. Proper execution enables you
to squeeze into the lane next to you, all the while causing
your victim to think the whole thing was his idea. You
accomplish your goal, and he spends the rest of the day
feeling good about himself. Win-win.

The Morse Honk

Honking is the new Morse code. You're able to communicate your emotions with incredible detail, just by varying your honk length, frequency, and the part of your hand you use. For instance, any heel-of-the-hand single honk under one second? Friendly salutation. Exceeding three seconds with an open palm? Desire to punch another driver in the neck.

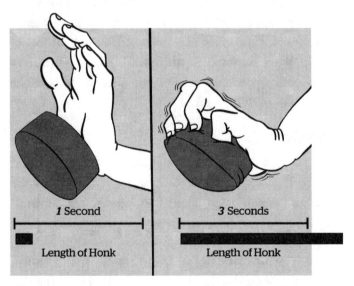

1 Second	*3* Seconds
Length of Honk	Length of Honk
Friendly salutation.	!!!*%#*@#?*%!!!

The Vanity Plate

The longest line you'll ever stand in is at the DMV. You're guaranteed to experience a gamut of emotions during your extended stay, including the desire to get a vanity license plate. I cannot stress this enough: This desire is foolish and fleeting. Acting upon your ignorant impulse to brand your car (and yourself) with KOOLKAT will cause you pain and paralyzing regret for years to come.[6]

Acknowledge Greatness When You See It

Before you get mad at someone for cutting you off in traffic, you need to pause and, at least for a second or two, try to appreciate what just happened. Chances are, if you had just executed that move, you'd not only justify it, but congratulate yourself for pulling it off: "I can't believe I just fit my car in that shopping cart–sized gap going 80 miles per hour!" They too, deserve to be applauded. This tiny attitude adjustment has lowered my blood pressure by several measurements.[7]

The Thumbs-up

Now, in the instance that the driver doesn't deserve to be praised, don't be like every other driver and show him

---

6. Arguably more pain and regret than a lower back tattoo of a Chinese symbol that the tattoo artist convinced you meant "hope."

7. The perfect term to use if you're not sure how something is quantified (i.e., blood pressure).

what your middle finger looks like. Odds are, this guy saw nineteen of those before lunch. Instead, try an exaggerated thumbs-up. You wouldn't believe the ROI from this form of sarcasm. I can't legally recommend this, but the thumbs-up reaches its maximum potential if you can manage to get your entire torso out the window while doing it.

Hand Signals

If you're on a bike and you're banking on me remembering the hand signals I learned when I was fifteen, there's probably a collision in your future.

The Seven

This is a great alternative to the standard ten-and-two. It involves zero hands and one knee. It's a great way to drive while eating fries.

Golf Rules for the Rest of Us

....

Every time I play golf, I realize how ludicrous it is to subject myself to the same rules as professionals. When I go to a batting cage, do I crank it up to 96 mph and hope to foul one off? No. I do what everyone else does—dial it down to 55 and relive my glory days.

The vast majority of us suck at golf. We need to figure out a way to make the entire experience better; thus, Golf Rules for the Rest of Us:

- ○ When you hit a ball into the woods, just find a ball. It doesn't have to be your ball—any white ball will do.

- ○ Each player gets one mulligan per dollar spent on greens fees. $60 = 60 mulligans. When a player runs out of mulligans, he is allowed to start using do-overs (players get sixty of those as well).

- ○ The red tees are there for a reason. Use them. Some would say they're for women and children, but those people also shoot in the mid-70s and wear Musk deodorant.

- ○ First person to point out that the guy who plumb bobs before a putt actually doesn't even know what

that does gets to move his own ball eight feet closer to the hole. The plumb bobber must then putt with his 8-iron, left-handed.

○ Players who discover upon arriving at the first tee that the course is Cart Path Only today are free to return to the clubhouse and get their money back. No one should be subjected to those conditions.

○ Any form of "Hit it, Alice" after another player comes up short on a putt results in a two-stroke penalty for the perpetrator, as well as a hearty lower back slap.

○ If a player duffs a chip shot in the woods and no one is there to see it, did he really duff his chip shot? The answer is no. It was just a practice swing.

○ No player should feel guilty for quitting after 14 holes. Everyone knows that is the ideal length of a round of golf.

○ If an amateur player adamantly swears he can tell the difference between brands of golf balls, he will receive a three-stroke penalty for lying and must give each of the other players a sleeve of golf balls.

○ Not only is a player allowed to ground his club in a sand trap, but he is also allowed to build a waist-high sand mound to place his ball on if he desires. Also, if he'd rather not get sandy, he is allowed to take his ball out of the trap and put it in the fairway.

○ If a player has never legitimately broken 100, he has no right to get mad after a bad shot. That's just what he does when he plays golf. He hits bad shots. And he, my friend, is why this list was created in the first place.

Quit These Things

Barbwire Tattoos

In addition to their "always use clean needles" guideline, I think all tattoo parlors should establish another policy—a mandatory "Are you sure about this?" whenever someone requests a barbwire tattoo around their bicep. It would cause some much-needed second-guessing and clear the parlors from any liability when the newly barbwired hot shot comes to his senses.

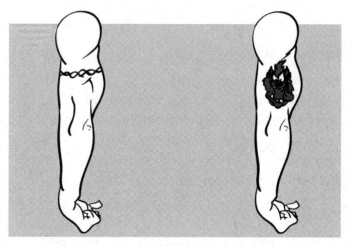

You have the same tattoo as Pamela Anderson.

How did this even happen?

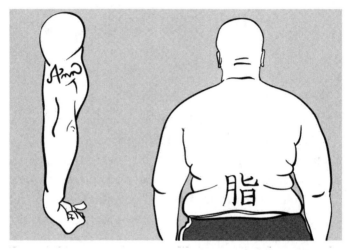

No one is this important.

Way too trusting of tattoo artist's knowledge of Japanese.

ChapStick

Let's use some discretion when we're applying this stuff, men. Nothing is more distracting than when you show up to our business meeting with freshly glossed lips. You see Linda sitting next to you? Yeah, her lips look less lip-sticky than yours. I vote we only use ChapStick in the privacy of our own homes.

Turtlenecks

When it's cold outside, there's an important decision to be made. You're either going to sacrifice neck warmth or sacrifice dignity. Don't think you're able to salvage both.

The minute you put that turtleneck on, you're entering a new social status that I'm pretty sure you want to avoid.

Musk Deodorant

You do know there are new smell varieties, don't you? Rule of thumb: When you're in the deodorant aisle, try steering clear of anything with a bronze/copper color. You'd be better off buying a clear-solid stick of BO than continuing on with the musk.

Over-the-Ankle Ankle Socks

I can't believe there's still a market for these. Is it a modesty issue that I'm not aware of? Is there an army of dads that are embarrassed to show their ankles? I mean, they've seen the no-show socks. The packages are right next to each other.

Music Faces

．．．

Lately I've noticed that there are a number of facial expressions that make their way into almost every musical setting. Whether you're actually in the band or merely a spectator at the event, you're sure to witness these five faces all around you.

The Lead Guitarist

Call me naive, but does playing a lead guitar solo hurt your fingers? Your wrists? It's got to hurt something. I can't think of any other explanation for the faces you're making. I'm a big John Mayer fan, but I'll only go see him in concert if I'm guaranteed to sit in the nosebleed section. I just can't bear to watch his exaggerated grimaces up close.

The Pain-Stricken Eye Closer

Why does passion so oftentimes look painful? I don't know—maybe it is painful. Maybe I've just never been truly passionate about something before.

The Brow Raiser

Apparently there's only one way to hit those really high notes, and it involves trying to connect your eyebrows to your hair. I caught a glimpse of myself doing it in the car one day while trying to hit a sweet falsetto and the embarrassment alone almost killed me (well, that and the near collision that resulted from me staring at myself in the rearview for twenty-plus seconds). I've since decided to only sing bass.

The Bottom Lip Biter

This face is usually reserved for drummers, and might be the sole reason I get distracted at concerts after about the fourth song. All of my attention becomes fixed on the lip bite. I start to wonder if he's going to bite clear through it, and if the band has a protocol in place if that were to happen.

The Bass Face

Ninety-seven percent of all bassists that I've seen performing look like they're in deep thought about something entirely separate from what is happening onstage. If you stare long enough, you can almost make out what they're thinking: *Did I leave the iron on? F, F, B Flat, B Flat. I don't think I did. C, G Minor, C, G Minor. My house better not be engulfed in flames when I get home, damn it. B Flat, G Minor. Does homeowner's insurance cover something like this? C, C. I am so screwed. Why does this kind of stuff—G Minor, B Flat—always happen to me? F.*

Ratings We All Pretend to Understand

Dow Jones Industrial Average

Telling me the Dow just dropped another 100 points has the same effect on me as telling me my winter coat just improved by fifteen muggle-duggs. I'm not even close to understanding you, but I'll still manage to muster up some level of concern.

Karats

If you're a person who A) understands the gold/diamond karat rating system, and B) cares a lot about that rating system, our families probably won't be vacationing together.

Airport Security Level

Has anyone besides a CNN news anchor ever thought about this rating system? Has it changed a single travel plan?

                        GARY
            Sorry boss. I know there's
            that big meeting in Detroit on
            Thursday that you want me to go

```
to, but I don't know if you've
heard—
     (whispers)
—the threat level is magenta. I
just don't feel comfortable fl-

          BOSS
You're fired.
```

PG-13

I vote we eliminate the current movie rating system and re-place it with the answer to this simple question: Will watching this movie with your in-laws cause an awkwardness-induced full-body sweat at any point? Yes or no?

Sea Level

I think geographers are just screwing with us on this. There can't really be a way to know this, can there?

Nielsen Ratings

In doing some Wikipedia research to make a good joke here, I learned that the CNBC show *McEnroe* received a 0.0 rating . . . twice. I still don't understand what that means, but I'm certain it's laughable.

IQ

This one always trips me up a bit.

> NEIL
> See that guy over there? Guess
> what his IQ is?

> ME
> 760?

> NEIL
> No. 150.

> ME
> Pssh. Idiot.

> NEIL
> Actually, that makes him a
> certified genius.

> ME
> Oh . . . yeah. I knew—He must
> have nailed the Language Arts
> section.

QB Passer Rating

Any rating system that has a perfect score of 158.3 (seriously) leaves me really confused. When you're coming up with a new metric and you get to the end and you've defined perfection as 158.3, it's time to go back and rework the equation.

Shampoo: A Poem

By Tripp Crosby

This is the only way I know how to express my feelings toward my shampoo bottle.

You're the only one
Daily that I need
You're the only one
Daily daily that I squeeze
Without you
My hairy head
Becomes extremely waxy
I look like a different person
One who drives a taxi
Or if, even worse
I go two or more days without
My head looks freshly birthed
like I literally just slid out
Apricot Jasmine Mint
You leave the shiniest sheen
But what the @#$% do those things
Have to do with getting clean?
Now, compared to most women

I have very little hair
Still I fill my whole hand with you
It can't hurt, and I don't care
I like the way you feel
Slippery and Slimy.
Especially when your residue
Runs right down through my hiney
Twenty minutes later
After zoning into hot air
I can't seem to remember
If I already washed my hair
Oh well, it doesn't matter
As long as I still have heat
It clearly states on the bottle
it's okay if I want to repeat
And, my hair isn't all
That you are making cleaner
The longer that I lather
the cleaner I get each finger
Wait. Something doesn't feel right
This I can't believe
I somehow used the wrong bottle
What the heck is Summer's Eve?

General Tips

....

○ No one will ever be as impressed with your abs as you are.

○ Adults don't have ringtones.

○ You're not allowed to get mad at me for not washing my hands after using the restroom if you let your dog lick you on the mouth.

○ Having an opinion about everything makes us not want to hear your opinion about anything.

20 Ways to Make Sports More Exciting

....

1 In football, defensive linemen have to kick all field goals in the first half of a football game. Fourth downs are now a win-win.

2 Four times per season, hockey players must dress like male figure skaters for the entire game. Doesn't matter which four games, and both teams don't have to do it on the same night.

❸ In basketball, a bench shot is worth seven points. During time-outs, bench players select one representative to shoot seated bench shots until play resumes. Seven points per make.

❹ In baseball, every Tuesday during the eighth inning, all batters are allowed to hit off of a tee.

❺ In the PGA's FedExCup Playoffs, all players must play the third round with only one club. Doesn't matter which club they choose, but it can only be one.

❻ In soccer, players are allowed to be offsides during the last ten minutes of a tied soccer match.

❼ If a foul occurs in basketball, the foulee can either take the free throws or engage the fouler in a hockey-style fight for forty-five seconds.

❽ After a touchdown in football, teams can kick an extra point, go for two, or go for nine. The nine-point conversion starts at the same spot on the field as the two-point conversion, but there are twenty-eight men on defense.

❾ Instead of a tip-off to begin a basketball game, the home team selects an A-list celebrity to shoot a free throw. If he/she makes it, home team's ball. Misses it? The other team gets the ball and the celebrity has to give one lucky fan $20,000 and an autographed 8×10 glossy.

⑩ Every August 13 (Bear Day), every ballpark in America will have a wild bear roam the field for the entire game.

⑪ In every college football game, one of the footballs in rotation is filled with helium.

⑫ If a team wears throwback uniforms of any kind, they must be worn the way they were originally worn. Short shorts in basketball, leather helmets in football, oversized cotton jerseys in baseball, and so on. This must happen three times per season.

⑬ In tennis, second sets are always played opposite-handed.

⑭ Every July 4th, in honor of America's independence, baseball and golf will switch balls for a day.

⑮ Swimsuits are replaced with business suits in the swimming finals of the Pan American Games.

⑯ In NASCAR, laps 350 through 400 of the Pocono 500 must be driven while texting and/or tweeting.

⑰ Steroid Saturdays become a part of the Major League Baseball season. All teams designate one player to spend the entire season pumping himself

full of performance-enhancing drugs. He only gets to play on Saturday, but he gets to use a corked bat and his own batting practice coach to pitch.

18 One day a month, all professional games start at 3 am.

19 Teams are allowed to incorporate a mini-trampoline into two inbounds plays per game.

20 In overtime, normal field goals are replaced with paper football field goals. A table will be brought out to midfield and the offensive head coach flicks while the defensive head coach creates the uprights.

About the Authors

Tripp and Tyler are a sketch comedy duo most known for their numerous viral YouTube videos. They have been writing, directing, and performing comedy since 2005 and have since amassed dozens of millions of views. They currently reside with their respective families in North America.